A Musician

Three Months in Camp and Field

Diary of an Ohio vVolunteer

A Musician

Three Months in Camp and Field
Diary of an Ohio vVolunteer

ISBN/EAN: 9783337020279

Printed in Europe, USA, Canada, Australia, Japan

Cover: Foto ©ninafisch / pixelio.de

More available books at **www.hansebooks.com**

THREE MONTHS IN CAMP AND FIELD.

DIARY

OF AN

OHIO

VOLUNTEER.

BY

A MUSICIAN, CO. H,

19TH REGIMENT.

CLEVELAND:
PRINTED AND FOR SALE BY THE AUTHOR.
1861.

PREFACE.

———•———

The leading object of the Author of this small volume, is to give his readers a full and authentic account of the Campaign of the 19th Regiment, Ohio Volunteer State Militia, giving in rotation every incident of any note connected with the Regiment, from the time of going into Camp, till the time of the return of the Regiment to the State of Ohio; together with a description of all the Camps occupied by the Regiment, and, also, a full description of that part of the State of Virginia, in which, and through which the 19th made its long and fatiguing marches; and, also, a description of the manners, customs and appearance of the people of Western Virginia. The Author hopes that the trouble and expense, he has been to, to collect these notes and facts, may meet the approbation of the people of the glorious old Buckeye State.

SALEM, Columbiana County, Ohio.

DIARY.

TUESDAY, MAY 14.—Our Company (Company H,) left Salem this morning at 4 o'clock, arriving at Camp Taylor at 9 o'clock, A. M., having a very pleasant trip. At Alliance, the junction of the Pittsburgh, Fort Wayne & Chicago Rail Road with the P. & C. Railroad, we were joined by the boys of Company E, from New Lisbon, and together the two Companies went to Cleveland, being lustily cheered at every place they passed. After arriving in Camp, the first introduction we had to the fare of a soldier, was our breakfast, which we took with a very good relish, after being about five hours on the cars. Our breakfast consisted of good bread and butter, boiled beef and pork, and potatoes, with coffee and other small articles, such as vinegar, mustard, pepper, &c., which I consider a very good meal for a servant of Uncle Sam. After we got dinner, we were shown to our quarters, where every man took his choice of bunks, and in a short time we were all making ourselves as comfortable as circumstances would admit.

WEDNESDAY, MAY 15.—The Camp was stirring, this morning, at 5 o'clock, our boys being, for the first time, aroused from their downy beds of straw, by the report of the brass field piece in our Camp. After stretching ourselves, and taking a good wash, we went to our breakfast, which consisted of precisely the same dishes that our first was composed of. The boys in our company are all well, with the exception of one man, who went to the hospital this morning with a sore arm. It rained nearly all the afternoon to-day, which made the Camp very unpleasant, and our quarters very uncomfortable. I will here describe Camp Taylor:—The Camp is in the incorporate limits of the City of Cleveland, about one and a half miles from the Railroad Depot, of the Cleveland & Pittsburgh Road, and a little South of East from the City Park; it is a beautiful piece of ground, very smooth and level, with plenty of good water, which is supplied from Lake Erie by the City Water Works. The grounds are surrounded by temporary board sheds, with two rows of bunks on one side, and three on the other, the bunks being about two and a half or three feet apart; there is, also, one end of the Camp appropriated to buildings, such as quarters for the officers, quarter-master and commissary departments, with a mammoth boarding house, where the soldiers all take their meals; the cooking being done by colored cooks hired for the purpose, one man having the contract of boarding all the troops in camp, at a stated price for each man. There is, also, a bank of seats at one side of the grounds, which I should think capable of seating five thousand persons. The grounds, I believe, are owned by the Agricultural Society of Cuyahoga Co., and is the place where the Ohio State Fair has been held, I think, at two different times. The surface of the ground is of a sandy nature, which, after a rain, soon dries up, leaving the grounds in good condition for drilling. There is now in Camp Taylor, abut 3,500 recruits.

THURSDAY, MAY 16.—The weather, this morning, is clear and cool, rain having ceased some time through the night, with a pretty strong Northeaster. We were awakened from our sleep this morning in the usual way, by the report of the big gun, after which we had the pleasure of listening to the Reveille, played by the martial band of Col. Steadman's 14th Regiment of O. V. M., which is now our neighbour in Camp Taylor. We took breakfast rather late this morning, our turn not coming till near nine o'clock. After taking breakfast, our company, along with Company A and Company E, went on drill, and was put through for nearly three hours, and part of the time on the double quick move, which appeared to give the boys an excellent appetite for their dinner. There were two of the boys of Company H deserted us yesterday, and made their way back to Salem, they having got quite satisfied with soldiering in one day. There was quite an excitement raised in our barracks this morning, by the accidental discharge of a pistol, in the hands of a German belonging to a Company of German Yeagers, from Sandusky City, the charge coming very near taking effect in one of the members of the same Company. When, after the excitement had somewhat abated, the Yeagers formed into line and marched out of Camp, turning their faces homeward, their Company not being assigned to a Regiment for three months service, they not being willing to serve for any longer time. Since the mud has dried up, the boys have had a great time at pitching pennies, and gambling on a small scale, that being the only way they have of killing time during the time they are not on duty. We had a fine battalion drill this afternoon, Capt. SAMUEL BEATTY taking command of the battalion.

FRIDAY, MAY 17.—There is still a cold Northeast wind, which makes coats and blankets feel very comfortable, although the weather is clear, and sun shining with considerable warmth. There was quite a number deserted this morning, some scaling the fence and giving leg bail, while others passed out of the gate and forgot to return. The boys are still standing around the fire, and shaking as if they had an ague fit; and those that cannot get near the fire are trying to warm themselves by violent exercise, which I think is much better than standing by the fire, which is made of wet straw thrown from our bunks, which you can readily believe makes a very bad fire. I lay in bed, or, rather, in my bunk, all night, and shook with the cold, but as soon as I got out and could exercise myself sufficiently to get my blood in circulation, I felt pretty comfortable. There was another Company left Camp this morning, they not being willing to go for more than three months, and the probability is, that there will some more go soon, unless they go into the three year's service. There are yet four Companies in Camp, that has not been assigned to a Regiment, as three month's troops, and if they do not enlist for three years, they will, also, be sent home.

SATURDAY, MAY 18.—The weather, this morning, is clear and cool, although towards the middle of the day, the sun shines with considerable warmth, which makes the boys look some more cheerful than the cold winds of the last few days. There was a member of Company G, 14th Regiment, died this morning, in the hospital. There are none of our boys in the hospital at this time, they all being in a condition to take their rations of pork and beans, that is, when they get the beans, they not being quite as plenty as the pork. Three Companies of our Regiment, Companies A, E, and H, marched out of Camp this morning, and had quite a fine parade in the grove, not far from the Camp. The Battalion commanded by Capt. BEATTY, of Company A,

Canton Light Guards, when, after two or three hours drilling and laying on the grass alternately, the Battalion marched back to Camp very much pleased with the morning's exercise. Some of the boys of Company H, received letters from home to day, the contents of which they appeared to devour with the greatest gusto. The Salem *Republican* was, also, received by some of them, and which appeared to be a very welcome visitor. We have had very good order in our Company since coming into Camp, with a very few exceptions, caused by the little too free use of the ardent; but I think when the boys get the wire edge worn off, there will be no more trouble in that respect.

SUNDAY, MAY 19.— The weather, this morning, looks rather lowering, but notwithstanding, there was three or four Companies attended church in the city, at 10 o'clock. Your humble servant did not attend church, having been detailed on guard duty, and had to stand regular watches for twenty-four hours, two hours on and four off. It commenced raining about eleven o'clock, and rained pretty near all the time, for four and twenty hours, and is raining still. There was quite a row raised in our barracks this afternoon, when the Company returned from church ; some of the boys were so excited that they had to be placed under guard; but I do not think that it was going to church that had the effect of exciting them to such an extent, but to the contrary, I think that it was staying from church, and going some place else, that had the effect of raising the excitement. But such was the case, that some of them got so wild that they had to be tied hand and foot, to keep them from tearing down their quarters over their heads; but such will happen in the best regulated families. There is preaching in the Camp this afternoon, but there are a very few attend, compared with the number in Camp; but I think if it was pleasant weather, there would, perhaps, more attend, than on such a day as this. The health of the Camp is good, notwithstanding the cold, disagreable weather; there are very few in the hospital, and what cases are there, are, perhaps, cases brought on by needless exposure, more than any thing else. There are a few cases of measles, and a few of billious fever, but so far as I can learn, there are none that is considered any way dangerous. There are very few places where there are as many men living in the same way, and in a way that is new to them all, that there is less sickness in than there is here just now, which speaks very well for the healthy location ot Camp Taylor. There is now in Camp, as near as I can learn, about four thousand soldiers, and more expected to morrow. There is now five Companies of the 19th Regiment in Camp, and the other five will be in this week, which will make the 19th full.

MONDAY, MAY 20.—The weather to-day is horrible, it has rained all day, making the Camp a perfect bed of slush and mud. It commenced at sunrise this morning, and has rained steady ever since, up to this time, five o'clock, P. M., and is still raining. There was two more Companies of the 19th Regiment came in to Camp this forenoon; Company B, from Youngstown, and Company C, from Warren, both of them are crack Companies in my estimation. I was glad to see, in both Companies, quite a number of my old acquaintences, which had the effect of making me feel more at home than at any other time since I left home. Companies B and C are fine Companies, and will make their mark if ever they have the good fortune to try their nerves on the Southern rebels. The Youngstown Company, Capt. Hollingsworth, is the most soldier like looking Company in Camp, they having been furnished, before leaving home, with good over coats, made in good military style, and, also, with good caps in the O. V. style. There is yet three Companies of our Regiment to come into Camp; and if I was going to judge by the places they are coming from, what kind of men they were going to bring with them, I would say, without the least hesitation, that they will be all as right as a brick, for as far as I know anything about the boys of old Ashtabula and Geauga, I know they are all right, with their hearts in the right place. The health of the Camp is as good as usual.

TUESDAY, MAY 21.—The weather, this morning, is clear and pleasant, being quite an improvement on the weather of the last two or three days previous. There was 1000 muskets arrived in Camp to-day, to be distributed to the 14th and 21st Regiments, which will leave Camp in a few days for some point in Southern Ohio, or Western Virginia. The 14th will probably leave to-day, and the 21st on Friday.— Two more Companies of the 19th came into Camp to-day, one from Ashtabula and the other from Geauga county, and a finer looking set of men don't happen to be in Camp just at this time. The Companies comprising the 19th Regiment are now all in Camp, and the probability is, that the Regiment will be organized and mustered into the service some time this week; and if that should be the case, we may expect to be removed from this Camp before the end of the month. As far as I can learn, our Regiment, after leaving this Camp, will be stationed either at Zanesville or Bellaire, until such time as we are ready to go to Western Virginia. The 19th is pronounced to be one of the best Regiments that has been raised in the State of Ohio; there is one thing certain, there is not a Regiment in Camp, that I have seen, that has, apperently, the same amount of intellect and decision that the boys of the 19th seem to be endowed with. The Regiment is composed of the following Companies, from the following counties, and principally from the following towns:

Company A, Canton, Stark county, Capt. Beatty.
" B, Youngstown, Mahoning Co., Capt. Hollingsworth.
" C, Warren, Trumbull county, Capt. Barrett.
" D, Morgan, Ashtabula county, Capt. Crain.
" E, New Lisbon, Columbiana county, Capt. Bean.
" F, Chardon, Geauga county, Capt. Paine.
" G, Akron, Summit county, Capt. Buckley.
" H, Salem, Columbiana county, Capt. Preston.
" I. Ashtabula, Ashtabula county, Capt. Hoyt.
" K, Cuyahoga Falls, Summit county, Capt. Konkle.

In the organization of the Regiment, Capt. Beatty was elected Colonel; Capt. Hollingsworth, elected Lieutenant Colonel; and the brave old Capt. Buckley, was promoted to the Majorship of the Regiment. There was a little incident that occured this afternoon, that I will mention here, showing in what kind of estimation the boys of the 19th are held, by the good citizens of Cleveland. While sitting within earshot of some ladies and gentlemen, this afternoon, a fine old motherly looking lady made the remark, that the 19th was the best looking Regiment that had been in Camp Taylor, when an old gray haired sire, who sat beside her, turned towards her and said, with all the warmth of a boy of twenty summers, "my dear, I would like to join that Regiment, and fight beside of them boys, for said he, I can see by the way they hold their heads that them boys will never turn their backs to the enemies of their country."

WEDNESDAY, MAY 22.—The weather, this morning, is yet pretty cool, although it is much pleasanter than it has been for the last four and twenty hours; the mud has pretty much all dried up, leaving the grounds in excellent condition for drilling, and at the same time adding much to the appearance of the men. The 14th Regiment left Camp Taylor this morning, for Marietta, Ohio, so I was informed by an officer of the Regiment; but I was informed afterwads, by good authority, that they go from here to Columbus, where they are to be uniformed and fully armed, when they will be sent directly into Western Virginia. There was quite an important change made in our feeding arrangements, this morning. As I have mentioned in another place, heretofore all the soldiers in Camp, took their meals in one mammoth boarding house, but this morning, all three months volunteers drew their rations, and the boys are now busily engaged in cooking their own dinner. The grub, heretofore, has been good enough, if it had been properly cooked, but the cooking has been pretty hard, so hard, that the boys began to growl considerable; but now, as the provisions are dealt out to each Company unprepared, the boys will have a fine chance to try their skill in the cullinary line; and if they cannot cook their grub to suit their own taste, they will have no one to growl at. Our dinner was certainly an improvement on the grub that we formerly had, the quantity nor quality has not improved, but there was certainly an improvement in the cooking of it; we do not get quite as much of a variety as we did before drawing rations; we have had our rations of butter, pepper and mustard stopped. Our rations, now, consist of bread, mess pork, potatoes, beans, coffee, sugar, vinegar and salt, which, if we get plenty of it, we will fare pretty well, but I think we will fare worse before the end of three months than we do at present. It goes pretty hard with some of the boys to come down to bread, pork, potatoes and such like, when they have been used to all the luxuries that the land produces; but it cannot be looked for in a military camp, if we get enough of the substantials of life, we can very easily get along without the superfluities. If a man cannot screw his courage up high enough to live three months on pork, beans, potatoes and bread, along with other little fixins to sweeten up with, he had better stay at home and not pretend to go a soldiering, for hardships may be expected, and what we think is hard fare here in Camp Taylor, we may, in less than three months, wish for as a perfect feast; therefore, I would say, be content when the cravings of hunger is appeased.

THURSDAY, MAY 23.—The weather still continues to be

very cool for the time of year; through the middle of the day
the air is quite warm and refreshing, but the mornings and
evenings are quite chilly, and the nights are so cold, that it
is almost impossible to sleep; our blankets being very thin,
and no way calculated to protect us from the cold; but there
is one consolation which we have to depend upon, and that
is, that this cold weather will not last all summer. The
Camp looks lively this morning, every one, apparently, being
busily engaged in doing something; some are engaged in
cooking; some in chopping wood; some washing their socks,
handkerchiefs, and other small articles of clothing; some
pitching pennies, while some are at the more useful occupa-
tion of reading the morning papers, and informing themselves of the current events of these troublesome times. I
sat watching the boys this morning, in their various occupa-
tions and pastimes, and finally come to the conclusion that
it would repay any one to make a visit to a military camp,
if for no other purpose than to study the character and disposition of men picked up promiscuously from every part of
the State. We have here the sober, straight faced, sturdy
christian; the sober, thoughtful, non-professor; the quiet,
unobtrusive, free thinker; the genial, jovial, smiling and fun
loving; the crusty, snapish, cur dog propensity; and I am
sorry to say, a very large representation of the noisy, cursing and quarreling kind; but I do not know that I ever saw
any better order among as large a lot of men than there is
among the soldiers in this place. I have thought that the
men instinctively are drawn toward, and sympathise with
one another, their minds being fixed upon the one all absorbing
theme, the upholding of our Constitution, the enforcement
of our national laws, and the vindicating the rights of our
common country, at least, most any one would think so, to see
the good feeling that exist among them, even among men
whose tastes and dispositions differ in every other respect;
but be that as it may, there is certainly a good feeling existing between the soldiers in Camp. The 21st Regiment is
making preperations to leave Camp to-morrow morning, I
believe they are ordered to Jackson, Jackson connty, in the
South part of the State of Ohio, at least, I see it so stated in
the morning papers. After the 21st leaves Camp, there will
be none here but the 19th, with the exception of three or
four Companies of three year men, who, I understand, will
be removed to Camp Jackson, at Columbus. I also under-

stand that there will not be any more troops quartered in Camp Taylor, after the removal of what are here now ; the probability is, that Camp Taylor will be broken up.

FRIDAY, MAY 24.—The weather, this morning, is mild and balmy, with a pretty strong breeze from the South, which I think will be very apt to bring rain before the week is out. The 21st Regiment left Camp this morning, on their way to Southern Ohio, or more likely to Western Virginia. The 19th is now the only Regiment in Camp, with the exception of some three year troops. It is now pretty certainly understood that Camp Taylor will be broken up, when our Regiment leaves. I have been informed, by good authority, that our Regiment will leave Camp Taylor the first of the week, to proceed to Camp Jackson, at Columbus, there to be mustered into the service, from which place we will either go to Zanesville, or to Camp Lancaster, in Fairfield county. There is nothing of any particular moment transpired to day, more than the marching of the 21st. The boys in our Regiment have their regular hours for drilling; we also have dress parade every afternoon, which helps to take up the time which hangs heavily on our hands. The boys are getting quite tired of Camp Taylor, they would like a change of scenery ; and I must confess that I would like a change myself, for I am getting tired of so much inactivity. The health of the Camp is good, there being very few in the hospital ; a few cases of measels being all the sickness that I have any knowledge of, after strict inquiries made from those direct from the hospital. The signs of rain is now so good, that I think we will have rain before to morrow morning; and for my part, I should like to see some rain pretty soon, for the dust is begining to be quite offensive, particularly when there is as much wind as there has been to-day. I have not been able to keep the sand out of my eyes all day, and I should like to see a good sprinkle of rain to lay the dust, if nothing more. The wind is very high this afternoon.

SATURDAY, MAY 25.—Old Sol makes his appearance this morning, his face looking fiery red, after one of the hardest rains that we have had this spring. It commenced to rain about nine o'clock last night, and rained for an hour or more as hard as it could pour down, the thunder rolling, and the lightning flashing with the most terrible grandeur. We had, also, a shower of hail during the evening. During the hardest of the storm, our barracks leaked so, that in a few minutes our bunks was perfectly inundated, the water coming in, not by drops, but by the bucket full ; the place where I lay was as wet as if it had been out of doors, in less than five minutes; my blanket and oil cloth being of very little use. It was quite diverting to see the boys shifting their traps from one place to another trying to find a place where they could keep them dry; but the most of them gave up in despair, and finally settled down and took the rain as philosophically as they could. But the sun is shining, this morning, with the prospect of having a fine day. The boys are rather glum this morning, and some of them are very much out of humor; some of them are cursing the mud, and the cooks are cursing the fire, the wood being wet, and not making as hot a fire as the occasion requres. There are, also, quite a number that take particular interest in fulmigating the strongest kind of anathmas against the smoke, the wood being very wet, and making a great deal more smoke than fire. But, I think, after the boys get their breakfast, and the sun dries, and the mud drying up a little, that their equanimity will be some what restored. The boys are now begining to realise the advantages and disadvantages of sleeping in wet straw, and under thin blankets, compared to sleeping in their own beds of down, and under good thick comforts, such as they have just left at home. But there is nothing like a man schooling himself to any thing that turns up, and at all times take everything for the best—there has never yet been a storm but what there was a calm followed—so I think, perhaps, that will be the case in this instance. There was some of the Salem folks here to see the boys to-day, but I was not acquainted with any of them, therefore it did not interest me as much as it did some of the others. Our Camp, this morning, had the appearance of a small Lake, dotted over with small Islands, or, rather, it had the appearance of a small plain, dotted over with innumerable small Lakes, every little low place being completely filled with water; showing, pretty conclusively, that last night's rain was something more than a small sprinkle. There has been about five hundred muskets distributed through our Regiment, so the boys are now exercising themselves in *the use of this noble instrument;* they are now going through the motions of shoulder, support, aport, present, secure, order, trail, shift, and all other little etcetera motions connected with the use of the shooting iron;

and I am happy to inform my readers that the boys take to it as natural as a three month's calf to a pail of new milk, or a sick kitten to a warm brick; in fact, some of them go at it as if they were old and experienced hands at the business. This is Saturday night, and the boys are commencing to black their boots, to be ready for Church in the morning, and I think that I will have to follow suit, the Company having a special invitation to attend Church, in the city, to-morrow.

SUNDAY, MAY 26.—The sun came up this morning with a clear, unclouded sky, but before nine o'clock in the morning, it commenced to rain, and rained pretty much all the forenoon. Although it rained nearly all the morning, some of the Companies attended Church in the city, but our Company did not turn out, although a special invitation had been extended to the Company. Two of the boys of Company H had a bit of a fight this morning, one of them getting a beautiful pair of black eyes, and both of them getting a free pass to the guard house, they having the honor of being escorted to that very distinguished place by the bigest man in the Camp. About 12 o'clock, M., the sun made its appearance. and we had a beautiful afternoon. There was preaching in Camp at 3 o'clock, a very good sermon being preached by a Minister of the Episcopalian Church. I could not get close enough to hear the text, but the sermon treated on the duties of a good soldier, the minister making some very happy hits, and making some good comparisons between the soldiers of the Cross of Christ, and soldiers engaged in the present contest, that is convulsing this, our once happy country, from the banks of the majestic St. Lawrence to the golden shores of the Pacific Ocean. He showed, conclusively, to my mind, that the instigators and perpetrators of this wicked rebellion are carrying on their hell-begotten work directly in opposition to all divine, as well as to all human laws. In fact, he preached a sermon that any one who heard him would say, came from the heart of a good christian, and was delivered in a good christian spirit. After the service was over, there was sang, I presume by the choir of the Episcopal Church, accompanied by some of the instruments of our Regimental, Leland's Band, the Star Spangled Banner, and I think that I never heard sweeter or more impressive music in all my life. There is something that always appeared so soul-inspiring to me in that good old National Anthem, that

it was always a favorite of mine; but the way it was performed, and the circumstances under which it was performed
to-day, made me feel perfectly elated. After the anthem
was finished, the Regiment formed into line across the field,
when, after going through the exercise required at dress
parade, the Regiment broke into plattoons by Companies, and
passed in review before the officers commanding the Camp,
passing twice around the field, and then wheeling into line
as before we started. It is now pretty conclusive, that we
leave this place on Tuesday morning.

MONDAY, MAY 27.—The weather, this morning, is perfectly miscrable. Last night we had such a storm as we do
not have in these parts every day, nor need we want to.—
Some time in the night I was awakened from my sleep by
peal after peal of the heaviest thunder that I have heard
for many a day, accompanied by the most vivid lightning
immaginable ; when, soon after, the rain began to descend in
torrents, and continued for hours, coming through the roof of
our sheds and drenching us to the skin in less time than it
has taken me to write these lines. Our quarters, this morning, look worse than a horse stable, there not being a dry
place in it. We are a pretty hard looking crew this morning, with wet britches, wet shirts, and wet blankets, and not
least, but last, wet skins and no place to dry them. The rain
is still coming down this morning, not in such quantities as
it did last night, but enough to keep us wet and our fires
from burning; and at the same time, the wind is blowing a
perfect gale, making the rain fly, the smoke fly, the fire fly,
and, also, making our tin pans and tin cups fly every time
we attempt to put one on the table. There was, for awhile,
that the prospect for breakfast looked rather bilious, but we
have, finally, been successful in getting a couple of camp
kettles full of coffee made, and every man took his bread
and coffee and broke for the best cover he could find, entirely
abandoning the idea of taking breakfast around our table,
as we had usually done. The Regiment received orders this
evening, to leave this place to-morrow morning ; the orders
are to prepare twenty-four hours rations, and be ready to
march out of Camp at 6 o'clock in the morning. We go from
here to Camp Jackson, at Columbus, but what the programme
will be after we get to that place, I am not prepared to say.
The rain has ceased, yet still the sky looks rather threatening, and I would not be much surprised if we would have

more rain before morning, but I hope not, for I would like
to sleep some to-night, being that we have to be on the move
all day to-morrow. The Companies have drawn their rations,
and the cooks are now busily engaged in cooking them. Our
boys all feel good over the orders to leave Camp Taylor, but
it is more than likely that we will not find as good quarters
the next place we stop at; but there is nothing like change.

TUESDAY, MAY 28.—The weather, this morning, is clear
and pleasant, the sun shining with more warmth than at any
other time this spring. Every one is astir this morning,
packing up their dunnage, preparatory to leaving for the
Capital City. The Regiment formed this morning at 8 o'clock,
but there being so much to attend to, we did not leave the
Camp till nine o'clock. We marched to the Railroad Depot,
where there was a train of cars ready to receive us, when,
after the Regiment was all got aboard, which took considerable time, the long train of nineteen passenger cars started
on their winding way for the City of Columbus, at which
place we arrived at about 6 o'clock in the evening, without
anything taking place of any particular interest, except one
or two fights, caused by the boys taking on a little too much
of the ardent. After arriving, the Regiment was formed,
and marched up to the Capital Square, and marched once
around the Capital, I presume, to give the boys a chance to
examine the structure, as I did not see any one speak to any
man belonging to the Regiment. After being brought up in
front of the Capital, some few men and boys standing on the
steps, one man proposed three cheers for the 19th Regiment,
but the man that made the proposition had to do all the
cheering himself, which he did with a hearty good will,
swinging his hat and cheering as lustily as his lungs would
allow him; but, unfortunately, he had to do all the cheering
himself, not another man or boy offering to give the faintest
bit of a squall for the 19th Regiment. Columbus, Oh! Columbus; Ah! Columbus; Bah! Columbus. Well, after the
boys satisfied their curiosity, and passed their opinion on the
beautiful building, (privately I presume,) and also on their
reception by General C. and Governor D., their opinions
being expressed publicly, without fear or favor, the Regiment
marched back to Camp Jackson, where we were assigned to
quarters for the night, weary of our days ride and disgusted
with the City of Columbus. Camp Jackson is situated one
half or three fourths of a mile from the State House, and

2

North of the City, and is an inclosure of perhaps twenty-five
acres, covered with timber, with some board shanties with
some bunks in; with room enough to lay in, but not room
enough to sit in; with two or three wells of hard, brackish
water. The place is known to those acquainted in Columbus,
as Goodale's Park. Such is Camp Jackson.

WEDNESDAY, MAY 29.—The weather, this morning, is
clear and warm. The boys was called out to roll-call this
morning, before 5 o'clock, after which, we took breakfast.—
At 8 o'clock we was ordered out for examination, which, after
passing, with very few being rejected, we were sworn into
the service, taking the oath to support the Constitution of
the United States and State of Ohio; and, also, to obey our
officers, the latter requirement, I fear, not being complied
with by some of the boys, as it should have been. The mus-
tering process consumed the forenoon, when, after dinner,
the Regiment proceeded to elect their officers. The result of
the election was as follows:—Colonel, Beatty, of Canton;
Lieutenant Colonel, Hollingsworth, of Youngstown; Major,
Buckley, of Akron. We start to Zanesville at 3 o'clock.
having had orders to that effect. Our Company, also, elected
their commissioned officers to-day, the post of Captain being
vacant, occasioned by our former Captain being repudiated.
The result of the election was, for Captain, A. Stilwell, formerly 1st Lieutenant; for 1st Lieutenant,W. H. I. Hilliard.
2d Lieutenant, A. Campbell. At 3 o'clock, Eight Companies
of our Regiment took the cars for Zanesville, where we arrived at 6 o'clock in the evening, and proceeded to Camp
Goddard, the Camp being situated about one mile from the
city. Companies A and B took a train for Bellair, from
which place they proceed on into Virginia, to be stationed
at some point on the Baltimore & Ohio Railroad, I believe
at Glover's Gap, or some place near there. Camp Goddard
is situated one mile from the City of Zanesville, the grounds
belonging, I believe, to the Agricultural Society of Muskingum county. The Camp is a most beautiful one, being situated in a valley surrounded by beautiful wood-covered hills,
which are now robed in the richest and most gorgeous of
green leaves, there being a very strong contrast in its favor,
compared with Camp Taylor or Camp Jackson. The Camp,
I should think, contains about twenty-five or thirty acres, is
surrounded by a good fence, with good substantial buildings
which are now used for our quarters. The ground is sur-

rounded by a carriage way and trotting course, which, I
should think, is near a half mile round, the ground, inside
of the ring, being grown over with a luxuriant growth of green
grass. The Camp is well adapted to the use it is now put
to, there being plenty of room for the movements of troops,
with plenty of good water, both of which are very essential
in a military Camp.

THURSDAY, MAY 30.—The weather, this morning, is beautiful and bright, the air being mild and pleasent, and laden
with the smell of sweet, fresh flowers, which makes the place
appear a paradise, compared to the places that we have been
camped in before. I tried, in my yesterday's notes, to describe to you the location of our Camp, but I find, after
taking another survey from a neighbouring hill, that 1 have
not done the place the justice that its beauty demands; suffice
it to say, that it is a most lovely place, situated in a lovely
part of the State of Ohio. The Muskingum Valley is one of the
most fertile valleys in the State of Ohio, and Muskingum
county is one of the richest counties in the State, as it is one
of the oldest settled. Vegetation is at least one month earlier
than it is on the Lake shore. All kinds of vegetable are
plenty, lettuce, onions, radishes, peas and beets, all of this
spring's growth, are now in the market in abundance. The
City of Zanesville is situated in Muskingum county, on the
East side of the Muskingum River, about sixty-five miles
from its junction with the Ohio River. The City is a stirring,
thriving business place, and I should think contains from
twelve to fifteen thousand inhabitants, who I should take to
be an industrious, thorough-going people. The City contains
five or six splendid Churches, with good School Houses, two
first class Hotels, two or three large and flourishing Machine
Shops for the construction of engines of various kinds, and
of the most approved patterns. The City contains many fine
business houses, doing business on a large scale, beside any
quantity of retail houses doing a flourishing and prosperous
business. The City is connected, by a good bridge across
the Muskingum, with the town of Putnam, which is a flourishing place of some two thousand inhabitants, all in some
kind of a good, prosperous business. The town contains two
Glass Manufactories, three or four large Potteries, where the
very best stone-ware is manufactured in very large quantities. The town also contains some good Churches, and one
first class Female College, which would be an ornament to

any city. The Railroad facilities are, the Ohio Central Road, from Columbus to Bellaire, passing directly through the city, and, also, the Cincinnati & Zanesville Road which terminates here. The Muskingum River being navigable nearly, or quite, the whole year, is, also, quite a convenient means of transportation and travel to the good citizens of Zanesville, and to all the inhabitants of the Muskingum Valley.

FRIDAY, MAY 31.—The weather is yet clear and pleasant, although we had frost last night, but the sun is coming up this morning bright and clear, and in a few hours the frost will all be gone, and the air nice and warm. The boys of our Regiment all appear to be very much taken up with Camp Goddard, and with the City of Zanesville ; it is indeed the most pleasant place that we have been in, in more respects than one ; in the first place, we get better rations here than we did at either Cleveland or Columbus, and in the next place, the people are more sociable and kind than we have found them at any other place, every one taking particular pains to make us feel that we were among friends, the very best citizens being courteous and free in talking to the most humble of the soldiers, providing they behave themselves as men should do, at all times. The fine personal appearance, and the social qualities of the majority of the men of our Regiment has, apparently, made quite a favorable impression on the good citizens of Zanesville. The boys all appear to tink that as long as they have to stay in Camp in Ohio, that this is the place, above all others, that they would rather stay in ; but most of the men seem to feel dissatisfied, for the reason, that two Companies have been sent on to Virginia, while the balance of the Regiment are cooped up in Camp in Ohio. Our Company elected their non-commissioned officers this afternoon, there being a great deal of dissatisfaction, and the majority of the men opposed to the officers appointed by Capt. Preston before the Company left Salem ; but now, as the boys have got officers of their own choosing, I hope they will be better satisfied. We have dress parade every afternoon, that, and the delicious music made by our splendid Regimental Brass Band, under the leadership of the celebrated Capt. Jack Leland, draws crowds to our Camp every afternoon. There are two Regiments in Camp Goddard at this time, the 20th Regiment was here when we came, and is here yet, so that the 20th, and the eight Companies of the 19th make in all, at this Camp, about sixteen hundred men.

SATURDAY, JUNE 1.—The first day of June, rosy, balmy, fragrant June, came in on us this morning with one of those mild, gentle and refreshing showers of rain that we frequently have in this, the most beautiful month in the year, and which is, at all times, a harbinger of hope to the husbandman. The vegetable kingdom seems to be undergoing, as it were, a magic change, under the influence of the mild atmosphere of the last few hours, and which will be much improved by the gentle showers of this morning. Our Company, this morning, divided into messes, each mess having ten men in it; formerly three or four of the boys done the cooking for the whole Company, but after this each mess will do its own cooking. There was a report circulated in Camp this morning, by some means or other, that the 19th and 20th Regiments would more than likely be disbanded, the State having no use for any more three month's troops, they being more of a burthen than a benefit to the government. How the report got started, or who the author of it is, I could not find out, but it had the effect of raising quite an excitement, and a great deal of speculation among the boys of the Camp. For my part, I do not believe one particle of the report has got any foundation whatever; it is like most all other Camp reports, all moonshine, and not entitled to the least bit of credence. For the first time since we have been in Camp Goddard, I took a stroll through the City of Zanesville this morning, and I must confess, that I was very much surprised to see the amount of business there is done here, although I have been informed by some of the citizens that business has not been so dull for many years in Zanesville, as it is this summer, and I have very good reasons to believe that that is the truth, for some in fact, if not all the largest manufacturing establishments in the city, are at this time standing idle, the war excitement having thrown every thing else in the shade. I must here again say something more about the citizens of this little City of the Muskingum Valley; I have invariably found them courteous, kind and hospitable; there is no place that we have been, that we have had so much kindness shown to us since we have been in Camp Goddard; there does not appear to be the least bit of selfishness about them, their generosity appearing to have no bounds. It would naturally be supposed that their philanthrophy would be pretty near exhausted, but such is not the case. Although there have been troops quartered among

them ever since the marshaling of troops commenced, and
their generosity has been pretty severely tested, still they
are willing to give, give, give, and willing to do anything
that lays in their power to make the soldiers comfortable and
feel at home while they are quartered in their midst.   The
ladies of Zanesville, God bless their kind hearts and pretty
faces, have shown themselves to be true, genuine daughters
of freedom.   We have received from them substantial evi-
dences in the form of various little luxuries, such as we have
not had since we left our own loved homes, of the goodness
of their hearts, and the interest that they take in the welfare
of those who have undertaken to vindicate the rights of our
government and sustain the honor of our common country.
Long may they live to greet the gallant boys of the old
Buckeye State with their kindest and most bewitching smiles;
and may they live to see the enemies of our country anni-
hilated, and freedom established from the far East to the far
West, and from the chilly North to the farthest part of the
sunny South ; and then long may they live to enjoy that
freedom which their fair hands has so much contributed to
establish.

SUNDAY, JUNE 2.—This morning dawns upon us with a
thick, heavy pall of fog, hiding everything from view, and
making our Camp look very cheerless ; the grass and leaves
are wet, and the mud is laying thick around the doors of our
barracks this morning, which makes it very disagreable get-
ing about, but if the sun could shine on us for a few hours
it would make quite a difference in the appearance of the
Camp.   Our Regiment received their knapsacks, havelocks
and catridge boxes to-day, and the boys are now trying to
harness themselves up in their military accoutrements,
which appear to be a pretty difficult job, for some have got
their knapsacks on upside down and their catridge boxes
on the wrong side, but after they get them tried on I presume
they will find out where the right place is.   Some thirty of
the boys of Company H broke through the guard and went
to the city last night, and when they returned they had to
do the same thing over again ; but anything like an adventure, or anything that has any excitement about it, they
appear to like amazing well.   There is a spirit of jealousy
existing between the 19th and 20th, and particularly on the
part of the 20th, which is quite a source of fun for the 19th.
The boys of the 20th Regiment think that the 19th is the

favorite Regiment of the Camp, and that they have favors shown them that are not extended to the 20th, and when the boys of the 20th are on guard, if they can get one of our boys in the guard house they will crow over it for twenty-four hours; but our boys have got too sharp for them, and in place of the 19th boys going to the guard house our boys have the guard house full of the 20th boys half the time. Our Company, with two others, Company D, Capt. Crane, and Company I, Capt. Hoyt, both from Ashtabula county, attended Church in the city this morning, at 10 o'clock. There was a smart shower of rain this morning during Church hours, but we were detained but a very short time after service on account of the rain. The day is very warm, the heat being very oppresive, without even the faintest sign of a breeze. By the time we got back from Church the boys were pretty well warmed up, having walked fast to keep from getting wet with the rain, but completely weting our shirts with sweat. This afternoon we had a hard rain, accompanied with thunder and lightening, which I hope will cool the air a little, for the heat has been oppressive all day.

MONDAY, JUNE 3.—The weather this morning is much unsettled, and still having the appearance of more rain. Between nine and ten in the morning the clouds broke away, and the sun came out with a heat almost beyond endurance; and at four o'clock it commenced to thunder, and it was not long till we had as nice a thunder-storm as any one could wish for. Our Camp looks rather hard after the rain; there is a little too much mud and a great deal more water than is any way convenient, it having rained so hard that the water is standing in pools all over the Camp. There is nothing of any importance going on, the boys all being housed up on account of the rain, therefore there is a scarcity of news. There is one thing that I must mention; it is almost miraculous to see the rapid strides that vegetation is making under the hot sun and warm showers of the last few days. The health of the Camp is good, there being very few cases in hospital, and not one of our company being on the sick list, every one of them being in a condition to take their rations.

TUESDAY, JUNE 4.—The weather this morning is still much unsettled, the prospect being rather better for more rain than for sunshine. It rained nearly all last night, and this morning our Camp is in rather a hard looking condition, the mud laying around our barracks this morning in a black mass, nearly shoe top deep. We received intelligence that there had been a collision between the Ohio 14th Regiment and the rebels at Phillippi, Barbour Co., Virginia; the substance of the report is that the Ohio boys came off victorious with the loss of one man, while the rebel loss amounted to twenty killed and wounded and one hundred prisoners. The report needs confirmation, but I presume we will get the official account in a few days. Our Regiment is getting much dissatisfied, having to be cooped here in Camp in Ohio while other Ohio troops, not any more efficient than we are, are in Virginia beating back the enemy, and doing somthing that is an honor to themselves and a benefit to the country while we are here doing nothing but consuming bread and meat and killing time, have nothing else to kill, not even a shadow of a secesh to kick at, let alone the substance to shoot at. There were some of the boys out last night on a special duty, which they term chicken duty; they, however, were not detailed by the officers, but specially detailed by themselves; their object, as far as I could learn, was to see in what condition the hen-roosts was in around among the farmers in the vicinity of the Camp. I have not heard their report but I presume it is satisfactory to themselves, if not to farmers who had the honor of receiving a visit from them. All the information that I can give is that there were some of them that were rather late coming into camp, but I presumed they returned as soon as they were relieved from their duty.

WEDNESDAY, JUNE 5.—The weather still continues wet and disagreeable; it rained nearly all night last night, and is still raining this morning. The deep mud around our barracks is rather inconvenient; the men in tramping through it carry it through the quarters and carry it into the bunks, so that our bunks this morning look more like pig stye than anything I can compare them to. The wet weather of the last few days has had the effect of making considerable sickness among the boys; there were ten or twelve patients from the different companies of our Regiment taken to the hospital in the last twenty-four hours, four of the number being taken from Co. H. The prevailing diseases appears to be the measles and the bilious fever. If the weather continues to be as wet for the next as it has been for the past week I would not be much surprised if the hospital would have a great many more occupants than it has at present. A change in the weather now from the damp, disagreeable air of the last three or four days to good dry, wholesome air, and plenty of sunshine, would most assuredly have a very beneficial effect on the health of the troops now in Camp. There have been three deaths in our hospital in the last three days, all the victims being from the 20th Regiment. While I am writing, there are two or three Companies of the 20th marching out of Camp to proceed to the city to bury one of their comrades that died in the hospital last night, the same Regiment having buried two others only three or four days before.

THURSDAY, JUNE 6.—The weather this morning is somewhat better than for the last few days ; the sun is trying to shine, and if it was not for the thick heavy fog that surrounds us, the morning would be pleasant compared to the three or four mornings previous. But I do not think wet weather is over yet; I do not like the looks of the thick fog that obscures everything from view this morning, and would not be surprised if we had more rain before the day is over. The good citizens of Zanesville gave the soldiers in Camp a picnic this afternoon, the ladies furnishing the good things, inviting the 19th and 20th to partake equally of the luxuries so kindly furnished by them; but, as it happened, the 20th got the lions share, while our boys came out behind, not getting a smell of anything, while the boys of the 20th got enough to last them two or three days ; but I think they needed it worse than we did, at least they appeared to be in a very great hurry to get it. There are some of them, I should think by their looks, that are better calculated to eat pie and ginger-bread than anything they could be put to, at least it came very natural to some of them that I saw.

FRIDAY, JUNE 7.—There was another heavy shower of rain this morning about three o'clock, and if I am not mistaken, there will be more before the sun goes down ; the atmosphere this morning is warm and sultry which is a very good sign of rain. The boys in our Regiment received to-day from the ladies of the city of Zanesville and Putnam, each a nice linen cap cover or haverlock, for the protection of the head from the sun ; we also received some nice muslin shirts, for which we tender our most hearty thanks to the fair doners. If there is one place in the State of Ohio that the ladies have made themselves conspicious for their kind consideratio toward the brave volunteers, that place is the City of Zanesville. The soldiers that have had the good fortune to be stationed at Camp Goddard, should cherish with grateful hearts the remembrance of these noble ones that came forward with loving hearts and open hands, and relieved their many wants, and added a great many necessary articles to make them as comfortable as possible. Long may they live to enjoy the reputnation they have gained by their kindness towards the de erving.

SATURDAY, JUNE 8.—The wether looks more settled this morning than it has for the last week, the sun came up bright and clear, with a fair prospect of having a pleasant day. 6 o'clock, P. M. This has been one of the finest days we have had for the last eight days ; we have had plenty of sunshine, with a good cool breeze all day, which had the effect of making every thing and every body look gay and cheerful.— There is quite a scarcity of news to-day, there being nothing going on except the regular old routine of eat and drill, eat and drill, eat, drill and sleep, with the intervals between filled up by playing cards and pitching pennies, which is the only pastime that some of the boys appear to think at all worthy of consideration, altho' there is quite a number that prefer reading the news or anything else they can get hold of.

SUNDAY, JUNE 9.—The weather this morning is clear and warm, without any signs of immediate change. The health of the camp is improved, in the last few days, there not being any sent to the hospital for some time ; and some returning from it. The boys have got up the old topic again this morning, the question being, What is to be done with the 19th Regiment ? Some wag, no doubt, started the report in Camp this morning to the effect that the 19th would certainly be disbanded and sent home, unless they enlisted for three years or during the war. The report has had the effect of raising a great deal of excitement, but I think if the boys would keep a little cool, and look at the thing in a reasonable way, they would see directly that there is no foundation whatever for such reports, and that they are only worrying themselves for nothing ; at least that is my opinion of the whole matter. The Regiment is now fully armed and nearly fully uniformed, and it is not very likely that the Government would have gone to the trouble to do that much, and then send us home without doing anything to pay for all the expense that it has been to. For my part I think the thing looks perfectly preposterous viewed in that kind of light; my opinion is that if we only have a little patience, (an article that some of the boys are entirely destitute of,) that we will have plenty to do inside of three months.

MONDAY, JUNE 10.—The weather is yet clear and pleasant, and plenty warm enough for the season. The grain in this part of the State looks unusually fine for this time of year, and all kinds of vegetation is coming to perfection with the most rapid strides. There is still considerable sickness in Camp, and I fear that if we have to stay here much longer that it will be on the increase, instead of decreasing, as I hoped it would, when the wet weather was over. Our Camp is beginning to have a very bad smell, particularly in the morning and evening. It is nothing more than natural that there would be more or less offensive smells about a place where there is so many men living together, in such a small space of ground, and particularly where there is so much offal of every description thrown promiscuously round the Camp. You may look most any way, and you will see decayed meat, vegetables, and every thing else that is offensive, and which is well calculated to create malaria; and if the hot weather continue, and the Camp is not cleansed in some way or other, I would just as leave be some place else as here.

TUESDAY, JUNE 11.—The weather is still clear and warm, a little too warm for comfort. There are very few of the boys of the 19th in the hospital at this time, I believe only five, two of them being from my own company. More speculating on the disposition of the Regiment; the talk is now, that we stay here until the expiration of our time, when we will be sent home; but I have got tired of all these surmises, and for my part intend to take things as they come, be they good or bad. Our Drum and Fife Majors, with some others of the martial band, waited on our Colonel yesterday and asked for a discharge from the service, there not being the least use for us here, but the Colonel said no; which convinces me that we are not going either to disband or stay here all summer. I think that it is more than likely that we will be here perhaps two weeks yet, and then, if I am not much mistaken, we will be very apt to see either Virginia or Maryland. Time will tell all things.

WEDNESDAY, JUNE 12.—The weather has been somewhat

changeable the last twelve hours; we had some pretty smart showers of rain during the night, but the sun is shining again this morning with a fierceness hardly to be borne. There has nothing of any importance happened in Camp for the last four and twenty hours, the regular old routine of Camp duty being the order of the day, accompanied with the usual amount of card playing and penny pitching as an after-piece to the programme. Our Colonel is now in Columbus, and the supposition is that his business has some connection, in some shape or other, with the future movements of the 19th Regiment which I think is the case. We have not yet got our full uniform, and I think likely that this is the business the Colonel is attending to in Columbus. The boys are all getting tired of this inactive life that we are living now, and there is some dissatisfaction among them, arising from the fact that two companies are now in Virginia doing some good for the country, and gaining credit for themselves, while the balance of us are laying in Camp doing nothing. There is still some sickness among the men but not as much as there was a week ago. There are a few cases of sickness in Camp that have been brought on by drunkenness and exposure, which I think has been the case in more instances than one; then there are some who are always too sick to do duty, but every time they can get out of Camp they will go to the city, and run around for hours, and when they cannot get passed through the gate they most generally manage to pass themselves through the guard, and over the fence in double quick time; but as a general thing the boys do their duty with a very good grace, with perhaps a very few exceptions. The 20th Regiment is still our neighbors, although the intercourse between us is very limited, there still being rather a hard feeling existing between them, but never amounting to anything more then putting one and another in the guardhouse as often as they can find a chance to do so.

THURSDAY, JUNE 13.—The sun came up this morning looking red, fiery, showing pretty conclusively that we will have a pretty warm day. There has not been any change, or anything of any importance going on in Camp for the last twenty-four hours, the regular Camp duty being the special order of the day, interspersed occasionally with a few cases of drunkenness and disorder. Our drummer and myself took a stroll out of Camp this morning, and are now in a beautiul grove about three-fourths of a mile from the Camp, where we are both busily engaged in writing. I am now writing these lines in my note book, while he is writing something of perhaps more importance, at least to himself —for instance, a letter to his father and mother, or sister, or brother, or perhaps of something of still more importance to him, a nice little billet to his dear little dulcina, the latter I think being the most probable, by the sly way that he was doing the job; but be that as it may, we are both enjoying with a very good grace a roll on the fresh green grass, in the shade of the sturdy oaks that crown the top of the hill on which we were sitting. It is certainly a great luxury to get away from the noise and confusion of Camp, and away from the foul stench that assails one's olfactory organs every place he goes. There was a report circulated this afternoon that the Regiment would leave this place in the morning for some point in Western Virginia, which had the effect of making our Camp for a short time look like a wasp's nest stirred up with a sharp stick; every man had his knapsack packed and ready to move in a very short time. I do not know how much truth there is in the report, as far as leaving to-morrow goes, but I think that we will leave this Camp very soon, perhaps the last of the week or early in next week. Five Companies of the 20th left Camp this afternoon for some point East of here, but I could not learn their destination, any farther than they go from this place to Bellair; and the supposition is that they go to take the place of Companies A. and B., of our Regiment so that they can join their Regiment at Bellair, that being the place we go to when we leave Camp Goddard. But where we go to from that place I am not positive, but I have a very good reason to think that we will be sent from there into South-western Virginia, perhaps to Charleston, perhaps no farther then Parkersburgh.

FRIDAY, JUNE 14.—The weather this morning is clear and warm. The excitement raised in Camp yesterday of our expected departure this morning for Virginia has somewhat abated; the Regiment has not yet recived any orders to move from our present position. There is no reliance to be put in any of the reports circulated, therefore we will just have to bide our time, and take things as they come. Two more Companies of the 20th left Camp this morning for Bellair. Our Regiment, with our splendid Regimental Band,

accompanying them to the city as an escort, while at the
same time the 17th Regiment O. V. M., marched into Camp,
and is now making themselves as comfortable as possible
along with the boys of the 19th. The three remaining Companies of the 20th leave in the morning for the same place
that the other seven Companies went to. Our Regiment is
still expecting orders to move, but there is no certainty when
we will go. There has nothing of any note transpired in
Camp to-day more than usual, except the departure of the
20th and the arrival of the 17th. There was a report reached here by some means or other, that the government troops
have been defeated at or near Harper's Ferry, with the loss
of seven hundred men, but I think the report is all a hoax.
at least I did not see anything in the Zanesville papers this
morning relating to the matter.

SATURDAY, JUNE 15.—The weather this morning still clear
and warm, there being no apparent change for the last three
or four days. The health of the Camp has improved in the
last few days, there being but three or four of the boys of
the 19th in the hospital. The three remaining Companies
of the 20th marched out of Camp this morning, and will
proceed to Bellair, at which place they join the balance of
their Regiment that preceeded them. There are still the
17th and eight Companies of the 19th in Camp here, about
the same number of men as there was before the departure
of the 20th and arrival of the 17th. The 17th is a good
looking Regiment, much finer looking men than the men of
the 20th, although there were a few Companies in the 20th
that were as fine looking fellows as you would wish to see.
The 17th came from Camp Lancaster, Fairfield county, to
this place, and will likely leave here when we do. Our
Regiment received the balance of their uniforms this after
noon, which consisted in gray jacket, made in military style,
with the *E Pluribus Unum* buttons as triming; it is the
best article that we have received from government, some of
the other clothing not being worth the thread that sewed
them up. The boys have now got a full suit of clothing from
the government, but still there are some of them that have
not got any uniform, for their britches went to rags in less
than a week after they put them on.

SUNDAY, JUNE 16.—The weather is still clear and pleasant.
The long looked for and anxiously expected news has arrived.
Our Regiment received orders to be ready to leave this place

at 6 o'clock this morning, to proceed from here to Bellair.
The 17th received orders to move at the same time, to the
same place. At the appointed time the two Regiments
marched out of Camp and proceeded to the Railroad Station
to take the Cars for Bellair, the 17th taking the lead; but
after the 17th got aboard, and the train moved off, we found
that we had to take passage on board of a train of stock
cars or stay where we were. Our Colonel concluded to keep
his men in Camp another day, rather than stable them up
like a drove of mules in the old stock train; so we marched
back to Camp, and put the day in as best we could till 6
o'clock in the evening, at which time we got a train of passenger cars on which we embarked and made our way to
Bellair, arriving at that place at 2 o'clock in the morning,
without any accidents or any adventure worthy of note, the
boys all pretty tired of their night's ride. After the boys
got out of the cars, the Regiment formed and marched to
their barracks prepared for them, which was nothing more
or less than an old Engine and Car House, fixed up for the
accommodation of soldiers on their way into Virginia. The
17th Regiment getting here some twelve or fourteen hours
ahead of us, had taken possession of some Steamers laying in
the River, and when we arrived we found them ensconsed
comfortably on board these Steamers. I was informed that
there was ten or twelve Steamers laying ready to take the
two Regiments down the River, to start in the morning.—
This information confirms what I mentioned three or four
days ago, that I thought we would be sent into South-western Virginia.

MONDAY, JUNE 17.—The weather this morning is still
clear and pleasant, without the least sign of any change at
least for some time. There is quite a stirring time here this
morning. There are three Regiments here, that is, at Bellair
and Benwood. Benwood is opposite Bellair, on the Virginia
side of the river. The boys have a fine view of "Dixie's
Land" this morning, all of them appearing to be anxious
to get their feet on Southern soil, although there is no
secesh in this part of Virginia. Companies A. and B. are
here, having been here for some time awaiting the arrival of
the Regiment. Our Regiment is now all together, and will
all move together when we leave this place. I think by the
looks of things that the 19th is going to make a pretty long
trip before their time of service expires. There are any

amount of army stores being shipped here this morning, such as provisions, horse feed, amunition, and everything that is necessary for a campaign among the mountains of Virginia. The boys are all in good spirits and appear to enjoy their expected trip down the beautiful Ohio. This place is called Camp Jefferson, but is nothing more then a distributing point, as it were, for the Ohio troops on their way to Virginia.

TUESDAY, JUNE 18.—The weather this morning is yet clear and warm. The two Regiments are still laying here on board the Steamers waiting further orders, and expecting to go at any minute. The 20th Regiment crossed into Virginia yesterday, took a train of cars on the Baltimore & Ohio Railroad, and moved off towards secessiondom. The boys are getting tired laying here, and want to be on the move ; and I think the sooner we get from this place the better it will be for some of them. There appears to be any amount of bad whiskey here, and some of the lads have been wild for the last twenty-four hours ; and I am thinking if they do not stop pretty soon, that some of them will begin to find snakes in their boots and bricks in their hats before they are aware of their presence. Some of the boys got so much bad whiskey to-day that it came pretty near killing them, when some of the boys seeing the condition their comrades were in by drinking the poison stuff, collected from the different Companies of the Regiment about two hundred, and went from one end of the town to the other, and destroyed all the liquor they could find. They poured out nearly one hundred barrels, cleaning out bars, cellers, drug stores, and every place they could find any of the critter.

WEDNESDAY, JUNE 19.—The weather is still clear and warm, without any signs of any change taking place any time soon. There are some of the boys look hard this morning ; some look as if they had been through the war in place of going to it, and I presume that some of them feel as hard as they look. The excitement over the whiskey insurrection had pretty nearly cooled down, but you may very easily suppose that the 19th regiment is anything else than a favorite with the citizens of Bellair. Our fleet of steamers left Bellair this morning and after a pleasant trip of ten hours we arrived in Marietta. Our fleet of boats is now lying at the wharf. Marietta is a pretty little town, situated on the North Side of the Ohio river and the West side of the Muskingum. It is in Washington County, Ohio, and is one among the oldest places in the State. Point Harmer, which lies on the opposite side of the Muskingum, is an old military post of many years gone past. It was a place held as a fort or rallying point for the brave old pioneers of Ohio, as early as 1780; and many a brave heart has left Fort Harmer, either to hunt the wild deer of the then Western wilderness, or the still wilder savage, that has never returned to his friends and his fireside, being killed and scalped by the Indians, and his body devoured by wolves. Such was the fate of many at that time.

THURSDAY, JUNE 20.—The weather this morning was clear and very warm. We lay here nearly all this day with nothing going on of any interest. It is very tiresome to lay around on a boat all day long, particularly when there are so many of us together. We left Marietta this evening, and run down to Parkersburgh, a distance of twelve miles, where we arrived about dark. The boys, I believe, were glad to get on terra firma again, having been on the boats since Monday morning. They all appear to be in good spirits, and the most of them in good health, there being very few cases of sickness in the hospital. We are now laying here in Camp Kanawha. The Camp is composed of a variety of accommodations, such as old freight cars, old saw mills, tan houses, carpenter shops, and most any place where a man can find a good place to pile himself down.

FRIDAY JUNE 21.—The weather still continues very warm; the heat in the middle of the day is almost suffocating. It is a great relief to get in the shade, some place along the bank of the river, for that is all the place that there appears to be any air stirring. There is now about 6000 soldiers in the neighborhood of Parkersburgh, and there are great preparations going on to push them further on into the interior of the State. Parkersburgh is the county town of Wood County, Virginia, and contains as far as I could learn by inquiry, about three thousand three hundred inhabitants. It is a neat place, there being some good buildings here. It is situated on the South side of the Ohio and the East side of the Little Kanawha river, and is built directly in the angle formed by the junction of the two rivers, the Ohio and Kanawha coming together at nearly right angles. The town is well situated for a place of business, the Ohio river the greatest part of the year being in navigable condition with

3

a good landing for large class steamers with a railroad in good running order from here to Grafton, where it connects with the main trunk of the Baltimore & Ohio Railroad, a distance of 105 miles from this place.

SATURDAY, JUNE 22.—The weather still continues dry and warm, or I might say almost hot, the mornings and evenings are middling comfortable, but from nine in the morning till five in the evening the heat is almost unbearable. Our Regiment is still laying in Camp Kanawha; the boys have fine times here, our Camp is on the bank of the river, and the boys have good times fishing, (making more water hauls then any other kind,) swimming and riding in the skiffs that are lying along the river. There are yet no signs of our moving from this place. The Regiment has regular drill every day by Companies, besides dress parade every evening. The boys have all been furnished with cartridges since we have been in Virginia, therefore it appears a little more like soldiering since we got full cartridge boxes and can smell gunpowder once in a while. Our night sentinels now stand with loaded muskets, and in case any rebels should show their ugly mugs we will be prepared to receive them. There has not a thing of any consequence taken place to-day, nothing more then the regular routine of Camp life being the order of the day. As far as I know, the boys are all well, there being only five in the hospital from the Regiment.

SUNDAY, JUNE 23.—The weather still continues dry and very warm. The Regiment is still laying in Camp Kanawha, expecting and awaiting orders to further movements towards the interior of the country. This place does not suit our boys, there is no secessionists here, and the boys are beginning to think that if they are going to hunt them and whip them, that it would be well to be at it and not stay so long here. This is Sunday morning, the first Sunday that we have seen in the State of Virginia, but it does not appear much like Sunday although there are some of us preparing to go to church, and the citizens of Parkersburgh are also making their way to church from every part of the town. I have not yet said anything about the Virginians. I will now give you a description of the citizens of Parkersburgh. In the first place they look very much like other people; in the second place they act pretty much like other people; in the third place they live much like other people, and in the fourth and last place, I think they are very much like other people; all the difference that I can see between the citizens of Parkersburgh, Virginia, and the people of Ohio, directly opposite them, is as I should think just about one quarter of a mile, which is about the width of the Ohio river at this place. There are no rebels here and every man you come in contact with takes as much interest in the prosecution and speedy termination of this war in favor of the general government, and the maintenance of the Union as any man in Ohio. There has nothing of any importance transpired in Camp to-day. The boys are all engaged at something or other to put in the time ; some of them are reading, some of them writing, some sleeping, some washing their clothes, some bathing in the river, and some playing cards, while the balance are standing guard. This has been one, if not quite the hottest day in the season ; the sun has shone all day with a perfect glare making the ground as hot as if there had been fire on it. There is no air stirring, it being perfectly calm which makes the heat a great deal more oppressive. Oh, for a good heavy shower of rain to cool this suffocating, heated air, that we have to endure for eight or ten hours every day, but this day in particular.

MONDAY, JUNE 24.—The weather this morning is clear and warm, our Regiment is still here in Camp Kanawha, but expect to move sometime during the day, the place that we go to from here is not known, all the information that I can give is that we take the cars on the south-west branch of the Baltimore and Ohio Rail Road, and start toward Grafton, but I do not know how far we will go or when we will stop, we received orders this forenoon to be ready to move at eleven o'clock, when after gathering up our traps and putting into our haversacks twenty-four hours rations, which consisted of six hard crackers and about one half pound of salt beef each, we stowed ourselves away in a train of old dirty freight cars ready for transportation to any place they have a mind to take us. We went aboard of the cars at about ten o'clock, but we lay there all day till six o'clock in the evening, the cause of our detention was there was a large amount of freight, such as provisions, horse feed, camp equipage, wagons, horses and all necessary articles for support and use of an army to be shipped on the cars and accompany the Regiment where ever the Regiment went. At six o'clock our long train started on our winding way toward the interior of the land of secession, rattle snakes, rough mountains, and bad whiskey, although the whiskey is no worse than in the State of Ohio.

TUESDAY, JUNE 25.—The weather this morning feels cool although it is clear, we arrived here this morning in the town of Clarksburgh, having rode all night in the old freight train from Parkersburgh to this place, a distance of about eighty-five miles, being under ground I presume longer than we ever was before, or will be again till each one of us has his own little underground habitation. I have often read of the underground Railroad of our free Northern States, but I never supposed that the Virginians had any such institutions, along with their other southeren brethren being entirely opposed to such improvements, I believe there is no less than twenty-three tunnels between Parkersburgh and Clarksburgh. Clarksburgh is the county town of Harrison county, Virginia, and is according to the decision of the Wheeling convention, to be the future capital of the State of Virginia. The town is situated on Tiger Creek and contains some four hundred inhabitants.

WEDNESDAY, JUNE 26.—There has been a change in the weather in the last twenty-four hours, it commenced to rain this morning about 2 o'clock and has continued to rain ever since; and at the same time the air is so hot and oppessive that it is almost unbearable. There is all kinds of surmises in Camp to-day, in relation to our prospect of having a bit of a fight with the rebels in this part of Virginia, for my part I do not believe we will see the face of a secession soldier for the next ten days, unless we get a little further from civilization than we have here. There is quite a large number of troops at this point. I think about six Regiments with one fine battery of field artillery ; the Regiments are the Ohio 3rd, 4th, 18th, and 19th, the Indiana 8th and 10th with the Michigan Artillery. The two Indiana Regiments leaves here this evening, accompanied by the Artillery to move on towards Buckhannon, the county town of Upsher county, where there is understood to be a rebel force stationed and committing all kinds of depredations. Our Regiment received orders this evening to strike tents and be ready to march at three o'clock in the morning.

THURSDAY JUNE 27.—The weather this morning is clear, and the sun shining pretty hot, we had a pretty hard rain last evening, but there is not many traces of it left this morning more than the few puddles of dirty water that we see laying in the road as we pass over them. We left Clarksburgh this morning about five o'clock and made our way toward the town of Buckhannon, when marching eight or ten miles we stopped and camped for the night, pitching our tents near the encampment of the Indiana 8th and 10th Regiments.— As this was the first march that the boys have had it went pretty hard with some of them; the Camp I have, named Tiger Valley Camp; and is nothing more than a Camp in woods on the south branch of the Big Tiger Creek, our Camp ground is partly on the Creek bottom and partly on the hill side; the Indiana boys took the bottom while the 19th Camped on the hill side which would have been a very pleasant place if water had been handy, but we had to carry our water about three fourths of a mile. This part of Virginia is not as well watered as one would suppose who never had been through it; the country is very rough and very poor.

Friday, June 28.—The werther is clear and warm, we are still lying in Tiger Vally Camp, but we expect to move on farther this afternoon; a fine Company of Cavalry joined us last night, they are well mounted, well armed and have the appearance of men that could stand a good many hard knocks; they hail from the good liberty loving city of Chicago and will be a formidable addition to our brigade; there was also three other Regiments of Ohio Infantry joined us this afternoon, the 3rd, 4th and 17th, or only a part of the 17th. Our Brigade now consists of the Ohio 3rd, 4th, 17th and 19th, and the Indiana 8th and 10th with the Michigan Artillery, and the Chicago Cavalry; making in the agregate about or something over 6000 men. Our Ohio boys are as fine a looking lot of men as there can be mustered together in any State in the Union; they are strong, athletic looking fellows with plenty bone and sinue and doubt plenty of nerve to back it up. The Indiana boys are also a fine looking set of fellows, who have apparently the right kind of stuff in them and will no doubt be the right kind of boys to fight by the side of. The whole of the brigade moves from this place together under the immediate command of Brigadier General Rosecrans.

Saturday, June 29.—The weather has underwent somewhat of a change during the last few hours, we left Tiger Valley Camp yestarday at 4 o'clock and marched 6 miles when we encamped for the night, it commenced to rain just

at dark and rained nearly all the night; there was some of
the Companies that did not get their tents brought from the
last Camp, the teams being sent back to Clarksburgh for
provisions, therefore some of the Companies (Company H
being of that number) had to lay down on the wet grass
and lay there all night exposed to the rain, the men in the
morning looking like so many muskrats crawling from their
holes. This Camp I have christened Camp Bullskin, there
being a small stream of water at the foot of the hill on
which our tents were pitched by that name. Some of our boys
killed three or four fat bullocks last night after we came
here, so if our waggons get here any time this forenoon we
will have some breakfast, but if they do not come before
noon we will have to wait and take our breakfast this afternoon, for we have not got either pots, kettles or pans to do
any cooking with, everything being left behind, at the last
Camp. Our Company waggon with the waggons of three or
four other Companies have just arrived, (9 o'clock, A. M.)
and the boys are now preparing breakfast. It is rather a
late breakfast hour, but the lateness, has given the boys a
good appetite which I think will pay for the long fast they
have had, not having eaten anything since yestarday at
twelve o'clock. After the boys got their grub this morning
a great number of them went to the creek and took a good
bathe, some of them at the same time washing some of their
clothing. I did quite a job of washing myself, beside taking a good bath, which is very refreshing this warm weather.
This afternoon we got orders from our Colonel to strike our
tents and carry them to the foot of the hill in a fine large
meadow and pitch them there which we did getting through
with the job just about dark ; and the boys feeling tired they
was prepairing to take a night's rest, when the orders were
to strike tents and be ready to march in one hour. The
orders came so unexpected that some of the boys made some
expressions that I will not mention.

SUNDAY, JUNE 30.—The weather is rather moist this
morning, it having commenced to rain about five o'clock
and still continues to rain moderately. The brigade moved
last night at eleven o'clock and took its course toward
Buckhannon ; the troops marched all night a distance of
eighteen miles ariving at Buckhannon at six o'clock this
morning. There was some of the boys pretty well used up
but still not half so bad as the Indiana boys, I believe there

was not more than eight or ten of the boys of the 19th that had to leave the ranks and fall back; but I verily believe that there was half of the boys in the two Indiana Regiments that had to fall back, for it appeared to me that every fence corner, stumps or log that we passed, we found some of them stopped to rest. We expected to find some of the rebels at Buckhannon but was disappointed, for not a rebel was to be found, at least none in arms. Buckhannon is the County town of Upsher county and is a nice, clean looking place, and I should think that every house had an ordinary family in; would contain from three to four hundred inhabitants; but the half of the houses are empty, all the secessionists having made a forced march to some other place, where the air is healthier than it is here at this time.

MONDAY, JULY 1.—The weather is rather unsettled, the clouds look thick and heavy, and the prospect for more rain is much better than for sunshine. Our Regiment is now encamped in Camp Buckhannon. Our Camp is at the edge of the village, on a level piece of ground, and is a very pretty place for a military Camp, providing there was not so many trees on the ground. This place is situated in a beautiful valley, the valley of the Buckhannon fork of Cheat River. The valley extends to the South-east and North-west as far as the eye can see. The width of the valley differs, in some places it is not more than one half or three quarters of a mile in in width, while at other places it is two or three mile in width. Our boys are experiencing some of the hardships that is naturally looked for at one time or another in the life of a soldier. Our Regiment has got nothing to eat nor have they had for the last twenty-four hours, it is pretty hard, but I presume if we can stand it for two or three weeks we will get used to it. We have nothing in the shape of provisions with the exception of a few pounds of fat pork and a little coffee, and I do not think there is any to be had nearer than Clarksburgh. Some of the boys are perfectly desperate this morning, and begin to think that if our quarter-master does not furnish provisions for us that they will have to call on some of the old secession farmers in the neighborhood and order them to bring us in a supply. Some of my mess-mates went out this afternoon and returned with some nice fat chickens which our cook prepared in his best style, and for once in forty-eight hours we had a perfect feast of chickens and corn dodgers, some of the boys having got some coarse corn meal by some means or other, for I had no curiosity to know where or how they got it, so that we got something to eat. There was a good many of the boys out on foraging duty this afternoon, and I took notice that they all came into Camp with something to sustain the inner man, some had corn meal, some hams, some mutton of their own killing, some chickens and turkeys, and some the regular old Virginia leaf done up in bundles, so you may think the boys will both eat and smoke to-morrow.

TUESDAY, JULY 2.—The weather this morning is still very much unsettled, there being much rain for the last two days with a fair prospect of more before the close of the day.— Our living has improved a little. Our quarter-master yesterday furnished us with some coarse corn meal, so this morning we are feasting on corn cake, fat pork and coffee, which is much better than fasting. Our boys are still bringing in some poultry and such things as they can get in the provision line which added to the scanty supply of corn meal furnished by the quarter-master make our fare pretty sufficient.— We received supplies to-day from Clarksburgh consisting of mess pork and crackers, and at the same time we received orders that no more foraging would be tolerated under a penalty of a court martial with a dishonorable discharge from the service, so as long as pork, crackers and coffee lasts we will be brought down to the old regime which we have been enjoying heretofore. There was a report in Camp this morning to the effect that the federal troops had captured the rebel camp at Manassas Gap, but there is not the least bit of credit attached to the report. The Ohio 3d and 4th Regiments joined us to-day, they having remained in Tiger Valley Camp when we marched from that place ; there was, also, a fine battery of U. S. Artillery joined the brigade.— Our force at this point now consists of the Ohio 3d, 4th, 9th, 10th, 19th, and four Companies of the 17th Regiment, the Indiana 8th and 10th with one battery of 6 pieces U. S. Artillery, and one battery of six pieces of Michigan Artillery, and one Company of Illinois Dragoons with one Company of Riflemen as body guard to General McClellan. Our whole force now amounts to about eight thousand five hundred men. I have come to the full conclusion that there is to be a forward movement made on some point, for the concentration of so many troops to this place is not all for nothing. There is said to be a large force of the enemy posted in a strong position some place in the vicinity of Beverly, in Randolph county, and I think by all appearances that our General is making preparations to make them a visit. The health of the boys of the 19th is not as good as it has been for the last ten days previous, but that is nothing to be wondered at taking all things into consideration.

WEDNESDAY, JULY 3.—The weather this morning is clear and warm; our Regiment still in Camp Buckannon. I heard this morning that as soon as the Brigade had a supply of provisions and other necessary supplies that is now at Clarksburgh awaiting transportation to this place, that the army will move on towards Beverly, and I think that all the manoeuvers that are going on here confirm that information. There is nothing of any importance going on in our Camp more than the regular amount of drilling, guard mounting, eating, sleeping and other little jobs that is generally to be attended to in a military Camp, with dress parade every evening, the boys as a general thing are in good spirits and taking events as they come as philosophically as they can. There is more sickness in the Regiment than there has been at any other time since we have been organized, and I would not be much surprised if there would be still more if we have to stay in this place any length of time, for I think that our Camp is in a very unhealthy location, being a very low piece of ground with a little too much shade and every morning pretty well surrounded with a thick unwholesome fog, with pools of bad water standing throngh the Camp. But there are supplies coming in pretty freely to-day; there has been a train of twenty or thirty wagons arrived, and if that many come every day the balance of the week I think that we will have a good stock on hand by Saturday night. I think likely we will move from here in the course of three or four days, or at least by the first of next week at farthest.

THURSDAY, JULY 4.—The weather this morning is clear and warm. This is the fourth of July, the glorious fourth, the National Sabbath of the thirty millions of the great Republic, the birth-day of our national independence, the day that is sacred to the memory of every true American heart, the day that every true patriot should venerate, the day that brings fresh to our memories the daring deeds of our patriotic sires of '76, and a day that every true son of freedom should venerate and respect as long as this great Republic keeps its proud position among the great and powerful nations of the earth. This day, eighty-nine years ago, Adams, Jefferson, Hancock, Jay, Henry, Franklin, Lee, Sherman, Morris, Hopkins, Quinnet and forty-four others of the sturdy old patriots of that day declared that this great country should be free. This day eighty-nine years ago our forefathers were contending for the freedom of these United States against tyranny and oppression from a foreign foe, and to-day the true sons of those noble old sires are contending for the rights guaranteed to them by the declaration of independence against foes that are far more unprincipled and dangerous than the minions of Geo. III in the days of '76, but may they, as the enemies of our country did at that time, be made to feel that the arms of freemen are long and strong and tyranny shall feel their power. At 5 o'clock this morning our Regimental Band playad the "Star Spangled Banner," "Hail Columbia," and some other national airs, that being about all the demonstrations made to honor this, to us, the most sacred day of the year. I have been all over the Camp this morning, and every place I go I hear the boys lamenting their hard fate of not being able to spend the 4th as they have been used to doing in Ohio. At 10 o'clock this morning our Regiment was formed into line in the street and inspected by the General. There was quite an excitement raised in our Camp this afternoon; at 3 o'clock the Regiment turned out for battalion drill, but the most of the Companies being rather poorly represented, the Colonel took one Company and went through the Camp and arrested every man that was not on duty, but in fact I do not blame the men for not being willing to do their duty, for half rations, bad provisions and much exposure is not very well calculated to keep a man's spirits up to the right temperature.— There is a great deal of sickness among our boys, I have just made inquiry and am informed that there are no less than thirty of the boys of the 19th in the hospital, and our doctor says if we do not get better provisions and more of them that there will not be a man in the Regiment in less than a week that will be fit for duty. The Artillery Companies of our Brigade fired a national salute this morning, each battery firing thirty-four rounds in honor of the the thirty-four stars on our national flag, and which is emblematic of the thirty-four States of the Confederate Union. There was another train of provisions arrived this evening from Clarksburgh, our post Commissary's department, is now getting pretty well filled up, so that in a few days I think the division will move from this place and proceed on toward Beverly.

FRIDAY, JULY 5.—The weather this morning is still clear and very warm. The boys of the 19th were sounded on the three year's question again this morning. It is said now if there can be one hundred and ten more taken from the Regiment as three year's men, the balance of the Regiment will be discharged and sent home. There was a vote taken I believe in each Company, which I think resulted in about one hundred and fifty expressing their willingness to go for three years. This division of the army is making preparations to carry on the war with great vigor, and along with other facilities there is now being put up a line of telegraph from Clarksburgh to follow the line of march as it proceeds on towards the mountains; the line is up and in opperation from Clarksburgh to this place, a distance of thirty miles, having all been put up in the last week by the 18th Ohio Regiment.— There is still a great many of the boys sick in the hospital, and there are many that ought to be there if they would do justice to themselves, for there are plenty of them that are still doing their duty and look as if they were hardly able to stand upon their feet. The dysintary has been pretty bad among the boys for some time, which has pulled them down considerable; it has been bad in the whole brigade ever since we left Clarksburgh.

SATURDAY, JULY 6.—The weather this morning is mild and pleasant, with some appearance of rain; we are still laying here doing nothing except eating hard bread and fat meat, not having enough of exercise to digest such food.— There is still much sickness in the Camp, and if we stay here another week and live as hard as we have for the last week, I am very much mistaken if we do not have more sickness than we have now; inactivity, bad food and exposure being most excellent stimulants for disease of which we have had plenty for the last eight days. The Camp, also, is begining to have a very bad smell from the offal and garbage that is laying around the Camp. I have not heard anything to-day in respect to the three year business and the discharge of the three months troops. There was another fine Company of Dragoons joined the Brigade yesterday, it is from Cincinnati, and is a fine looking Company, and is well mounted and armed, and will prove of service to the Brigade.

SUNDAY, JULY 7.—This morning the weather is rather changeable, we are having rain and sunshine in the same hour, and it is hard to tell just now which is going to predominate, or what kind of a day we are going to have. There is a regular row in Camp this morning ; it will be recollected that when our troops came to this place one week ago this morning, that our Regiment had no provisions, and the boys had to resort to foraging to keep from starving. There was an old secessionist came into the Camp three or four days ago, and made complaint to the officers to the effect that some of the boys of the 19th Regiment had visited his premises, broke open his house and robbed him of one hundred and seventy-five dollars in gold and a gold watch, when after making inquiries, it was ascertained that some of the boys of Co. C, Capt. Barret, from Trumbull County, had been to the place for the purpose of getting some provisions, and the supposed theft was saddled on to them, when after an examination and court of inquiry, it was decided to disgrace the Company and send it back to Ohio as being demoralized, and to send the eight men (1st Lieutenant of the Company included,) back to Columbus under arrest, there to be tried by a military court for a high misdemeanor. The Company was actually disarmed and started on their way home, but I presume that the General thinking that the allegations against the Company as being demoralized might be pretty hard to sustain, had them brought back and their arms restored to them, but the other eight did return to Ohio, where it is hoped that they will get a fair trial and be fully exonerated from the charge under which they are laying, and which I have no doubt will be the case when the facts are all brought to light. I was told by some of the neighbors of the man that should have lost the money, that he was never known to have that much money, and that he was unable to pay a debt to one of his neighbors, amounting to thirty-seven cents, and that the report was gotten up for the purpose, and with the expectation of bleeding the government out of that much money, he supposing that the government would refund the amount back to him—a pretty good secession dodge.

MONDAY, JULY 8.—The weather this morning is clear and very warm. We received orders last night to be ready to march at 4 o'clock in the morning; we were up and had our coffee and crackers, and was ready to move at the appointed hour, but we did not leave the Camp till near 6 o'clock. We then took our way towards Beverly, which is thirty miles from Buckhannon, and at which place, we expect to see some secessionists, if they do not leave before we get there. Our course lay nearly directly East and over the mountains, and through as wild a looking country as ever I saw. The roads are good in this part of the State; the road that we traveled on to-day is known as the Parkersburgh and Staunton turnpike, and is kept in repair by the State; the road is the most of the way made through the defiles and gorges of the mountains and is nearly all the time through a thick forest of trees with a thick growth of underbrush, such as laurels, briars, hazel and other dwarf bushes, which is a perfect hedge all along the road and which makes it almost suffocating to travel on, not the least bit of fresh air being able to penetrate through this natural hedge. We marched sixteen miles to-day, and camped on the top of a mountain. The boys suffered much with the heat this day, and two of them were sun-struck and had to be carried into Camp. The 3d Ohio Regiment being in advance of the brigade, on Saturday morning last, sent out about fifty men on a scout, when about half a mile East of here and at the bridge that crosses the middle fork of the Cheat river, they came in contact with about three hundred rebels which they engaged skirmishing with, and which retreated towards Beverly at the approach of the Regiment; the 3d had one man killed and three slightly wounded, and the rebels had (so I was informed by a member of the 3d,) three killed and seven wounded. Our Regiment is now encamped on the top of the mountain, half a mile from the middle fork of Cheat river and about half way between Buckhannon and Beverly, which place I have concluded to call mountain camp. We can stand in the Camp and look far below us, and see the tops of the trees that stand on the mountain side.

TUESDAY, JULY 9.—The weather this morning is clear and warm, after having rained nearly all last night. At 7 o'clock this morning, the brigade pushed on toward Beverly, with the exception of three Companies of the 19th Regiment that were left at this place to guard the bridge till the arrival of two or three Indiana Regiments that are on their way between here and Buckhannon. The brigade marched eight miles and encamped in the valley of Roaring Creek, and about two miles from the foot of Rich Mountain, at which place the boys got a sight of what they have been looking, for for the last two weeks—the secession army. They are posted on the side of Rich Mountain, about two and a half miles from our Camp and apparently in a pretty strong position. The three Companies of our Regiment, that were left at the middle fork bridge were Companies G, H and I, commanded by the brave old Major Buckley. After leaving Mountain Camp with the balance of the brigade, we marched down the mountain to the bridge and crossed over to the East side, where we pitched our tents and prepared to make ourselves as comfortable as possible till the arrival of the Indiana Regiments. After we had got ourselves comfortably fixed, the boys concluded to take a good wash, and in a very short time the river was full of the boys all enjoying themselves to their own satisfaction in clear and pure water of this beautiful stream, the water being so clear and transparent that you could see a pin lying on the bottom at the depth of five or six feet. The boys of the three Companies also took the advantage of the chance offered them and washed up their clothing while they had good water to do it with. Our little detachment is now encamped on the ground where the collision took place on last Saturday, between some of the boys of the Ohio 3d and a detachment of the rebels from the Rich Mountain fortification. This camp is also the place where the secessionists encamped the night after their hasty retreat from Phillippi, on the 3d of June. I have just returned from a visit to the grave of the man that was killed here on Saturday morning; I have also been to examine the bridge where the greasy thieves were concealed when they made the attack on the handful of the boys of the Ohio 3d, and find that the boys made good use of their muskets for the time they were engaged; they have put a great many balls through the siding of the bridge, through which they had to fire, the cowardly dogs, not coming out and fighting like men, but fighting through holes made for the purpose. There was one of the expected Indiana Regiments came in this evening and will remain here till the others come up, therefore, we will be relieved in the morning, and will push on and join the brigade. Our boys retired early this evening so as to get an early start in the morning, but the natural consequences of war are that it is hard to tell what an hour may bring forth. We had just got into a good sound, comfortable sleep and were

dreaming of pleasant scenes far away, when we were awakened with a noise that would almost wake the dead. There
was an alarm that an attack; our picket guard firing in every
direction, with the guard around the camp also firing the
alarm; but as soon as the boys got their eyes open, and
found out what was going on, and what was expected, they
made the best time in forming in line that I ever saw. It
was no more than five minutes from the time that the alarm
was given till every man was at his post with his musket in
hand and his hand on his cartridge box. I believe there
was not a man in the three compaies, except two, but what
was ready in the ranks and waiting for the appearance of
the enemy, one of the two being so badly scared that he
stuck his head in his haversack, so his tent mates said at
least; the other man was sick. The alarm was occasioned
by the appearance of a detachment of rebels in the neighborhood of the Camp, and the firing on them by our picket
guard. They had been sent out by Col. Pegram from the
Camp at Rich Mountain, for the purpose of destroying the
bridge, they not expecting to find more than our three Compaies there, not knowing of the arrival of the Indiana
Regiment, it coming in just at dark. Their intention was to
attack our little Camp and destroy us or drive us away, and
then burn the bridge, that being the orders that they
received from Col. Pegram. This we found out by some
papers that were picked up by some of the boys after the
capture of Fort Garnett; but they failed to carry out any
of the programme. When our pickets fired into their detachment, they killed three of their number which we also
found by documents picked up in their Camp after their
defeat at Rich Mountain, their great anxiety to destroy the
bridge being to cut off our wagon trains, which would be
the means of shortening our supplies of provisions and ammunition.

WEDNESDAY JULY 10.—The weather this morning is all
that could be desired, it having rained some last evening,
has cooled the air and made the road fine this morning for
a nice little walk of eight miles; at five o'clock this morning we pulled up stakes and took the road, when after
marching two and a half hours we came up to the brigade
and joined our Regiment. As I have mentioned before the
brigade or more properly division, is encamped in Roaring
Creek Valley about two and a half miles from the enemy.

48

The exact number of the enemy is not known, but according to the report of General McClellan after making the closest observations the circumstances would admit of, there are supposed to be from four to six thousand of them. They have destroyed some of the bridges in the vally, and between their Camp and ours ; which will have to be rebuilt before we can make an attact on them, but our boys are busily engaged at reconstructing them now, so that in a very short time our boys will have the pleasure of introducing themselves to Colonel Pegram and his crew of cut throats on the side of Rich Mountain. There were two or three Regiments of Infautry, with one battery of Artillery made a forward movement this afternoon but had to fall back on account of obstructions in the road which will have to be removed, the attack will perhaps not be made till morning. Our division is now pretty strong and is composed of the following troops, the Ohio 3rd, 4th, 9th, 10th and 19th; the 8th, 10th, 13th and 15th Indiana, with 18 pieces Artillery and two Companies Dragoons, and Sturgis Rifles, in all near 10,000 men.

Thursday, July 11.—The weather this morning looks rather gloomy, with a fair prospect of rain before the day is over. We were called up at 11 o'clock last night and ordered to prepare twenty-four hours rations and be ready to move at 2 o'clock in the morning, the boys tumbled out, started their fires and commenced cooking their breakfasts and, also, rations sufficient for twenty-four hours. About 3 o'clock the attacking column was in motion and proceeded to move on towards the enemies position. The officers appear to have changed their plan of making the attack, and instead of assailing the rebel camp in front and taking it by storm, as their first intention was, they made a circuit of ten or twelve miles and came in on the rear of their position, and would have taken them by surprise if all things had went as desired; but the rebels captured one of our Cavalrymen bearing a message from Gen. McClellan to Gen. Rosecrans, and by that means found out that our boys were marching on them from the rear which gave them time to receive us in that quarter ; they brought their Artillery to the top of the mountain, one mile from their main fortifications, and posted it in such a position as to command the point at which they knew our troops would have to make their appearance ; they also constructed a breastwork of logs and stone which gave them much the advantage in regard to position. Our boys reached the brow of the mountain at or near the hour of 3 o'clock, the firing commenced immediately on the side of the rebels with their artillery, but with little or no effect, they invariably firing over the heads of our troops. The Indiana 8th and 10th made the attack in front of the enemies lines while the Indiana 13th were posted on the extreme right and extreme left as skirmishers and sharp-shooters, while the Ohio 19th was held as a reserve directly in front of the enemy and in the rear of the Indiana 9th and 10th, and was directly exposed to the enemy's Artillery. The engagement now commenced in earnest, the enemy's whole line of Infantry and Riflemen pouring in volley after volley into the ranks of the 10th Indiana; in the mean time the Indiana 13th had silenced the enemy's batteries. The Indiana boys are still giving them round for round but begin to get impatient at having to fight a partly concealed enemy, they partly broke their line and were going to go into a hand to hand fight, when on seeing the intention of the Indiana troops, the enemy left their cover and prepared to meet them at the point of the bayonet, when Gen. Rosecrans seeing the broken ranks of the Indiana boys gave the order to the 19th to forward and fire, which they did with such coolness and precision that the enemy had to turn their back to us and turn to the bushes in double quick time, our boys following them and killing a good number as they were re- retreating. Our troops now have possession of the field and not an enemy in sight. I took a look over the contested ground and found that the enemy had sustained a vary heavy loss, while on the side of the federal troops was compara- tively light, but the work was only half done, the enemy was defeated it is true, but they had retreated (all them that were not killed and wounded) to their main fortifica- tion, and might be able to make another stand ; and which our officers all supposed would be the case. But our officers, thinking that the boys had done enough for one day, conclu- ded to take up their quarters on or near the battle ground, and wait till morning to give them another drubbing. Our boys lay on the bare ground all night, in a hard soaking rain, with their arms by their sides ready for anything that might take place ; but they were not disturbed through the night, but rested till morning, if it could be called resting. In the morning the boys were moving early, and making

4

their way towards the rebel Camp, but what was their surprise in coming in sight of their camp, in place of seeing long lines of armed rebels, ready to receive them, they saw but a few stragglers, about sixty, who laid down their arms and gave themselves up as prisoners. The whole secession force had abandoned their stronghold, and retreated through the mountains towards Beverly or Huttonville. The federal troops have now the posession of the strongest place in Western Virginia. They also have everything that belonged to the rebel army, tents, horses, mules, wagons, artillery, and a large number of muskets and rifles along with all their army stores, consisting of provisions, ammunition, clothing, and everything else they had. Their retreat had been so hasty that they left their private property, trunks full of clothing, carpet sacks and valises full of clothing, knives, swords, pistols; and even their private papers and correspondence with their friends was left behind. The number of killed is said to be by some 250, while some make the figures larger still, and others make the number less than 200. I shall be able perhaps to give the correct account in a few days. The number of wounded is small compared to the number killed; showing that our boys did not shoot altogether by guess. We took 250 tents, 100 horses and mules, 40 wagons, 4 brass 6 pounders, together with their ammunition wagons and magazines, with a great number of harnesses, saddles, bridles, and everything pertaining to a well organized and well supplied army. The number of muskets left in the Camp and taken from the prisoners is one hundred and twenty.

FRIDAY, JULY 12.—The Camp at Roaring Creek was broken up this morning and the Ohio 3d, 4th, 9th, 10th, and the Indiana 15th, with the Artillery, proceeded on to Beverly, while the Regiments that were engaged in the fight took possession of Camp Garnett, and will remain here till to-morrow morning. The boys are living pretty fat to-day on the good things that the seceshers left behind them; we are feasting on bread and butter, ham and eggs, maple sugar and molasses, dried fruits, preserved fruits, jams and jellies, cheese and crackers, and everything that is good, while some of the boys found a small keg full of old whiskey, which was good for the occasion. The boys are now collecting the captured property into piles, and there appears to be vast quantities of it of all imaginable kinds of articles, such as coats, pants, vests, drawers, shirts, socks, handkerchiefs, hats, caps, boots, shoes, with any amount of fancy and toilet articles, together with pots, kettles, pans, griddles, tin and wooden buckets, tin cups, coffee pots, teapots, coffee mills, candles, soap, and other articles too numerous to mention.

SATURDAY, JULY 13.—The weather this morning is mild and pleasant, with some prospect of rain. The last forty-eight hours has been the most eventful of the campaign ; we have met the enemy and defeated them on their own ground. Their strength in this part of Virginia is entirely broken; we have captured their Camp with all the appertenances pertaining thereto, leaving them entirely powerless, at least for the time being. Our boys are all on the move this morning, making preparations to move on towards Beverly, to which place a part of the army went on yesterday. The whole division leave this place, with the exception of two or three Companies of the Indiana 13th, which remain here for a few days, for the purpose of destroying the rebel fortifications, and burying the dead rebels that are still being picked up through the woods in great numbers. Their loss is ascertained to be much larger than was first supposed, many of them having died of their wounds after escaping from the battle ground, and are now being picked up by our boys and put in the ground. We received intelligence this morning of the defeat of the rebels by the Ohio and Indiana troops under Gen. Morris at Laurel Hill, and also of the death of Gen. Garnett. This was the last nest of the conspirators in this section of the State, there now being no regularly organized band any place North of Charleston on the Kanawha River. Our troops left Camp Garnett this afternoon and marched on to Beverly, where we arrived at about 6 o'clock, and where we proceeded to pitch our tents and make preparations for a night's rest. I will here give a description of Camp Garnett as near as possible from observations taken from three different points. The Camp is situated on the Parkersburgh and Staunton turnpike, twenty-four miles East of Buckhannon and six miles West of Beverly. It is situated at the place where the pike passes through the gorge of Rich Mountain, and where the road is commanded on three sides by high hills, on which the enemy had built their defences, and planted their guns so as to completely command the approaches each way. Their fortifications on three hills together, I should think, were near two miles long. Rich

Mountain is a range of mountains situated between the valley of Roaring Creek on the West, and the valley of the Valley River on the East, and is, perhaps, at its highest elevation, between fifteen hundred and two thousand feet above the valley of the Tiger valley branch of Cheat River. The range runs off to the North from Beverly and connects with Laurel Hill, and South from the same place and connects with Cheat Mountain, some twenty-five miles South of this place.

SUNDAY, JULY 14.—The weather this morning is rather cool. Our whole division is now encamped in Camp Beverly. Our camp looks like a city of miniature houses spread over the valley, and makes a fine appearance from a hill in the vicinity of our camp. Beverly is the County town of Randolph County, and is situated in the valley of the Tiger fork of Cheat River, thirty miles East of Buckhannon, and one hundred miles West of Staunton; the town is rather a rusty looking place and contains perhaps a population of two hundred and fifty inhabitants. I made a visit this morning to that part of our Camp occupied by the rebel prisoners, and took a stroll among them, and as far as my observations went I saw but little difference in personal appearance between them and our own men. I had quite a long conversation with some of them, and found them to be very intelligent men; and came to the conclusion that if they are a fair representation of the Southern army, that we have no mean enemy to contend with as far as knowledge and physical strength is concerned. I also took the number of muskets and rifles that we now have in our possession, taken at the battle and surrendered at this place on yesterday; the precise number is 876 muskets and 150 rifles, with the same amount of catridge boxes and belts; the number of prisoners is 823, including nearly forty officers of different rank. There is a detachment of our boys now forming to go a few miles from here to clean out a nest of rebels that are said to be a few miles from this place. There was also a small detachment sent out to open the road from here to Webster, to which place we go from here, and which is the place that we will perhaps start home from.

MONDAY, JULY 15.—The weather this morning is very unpleasant, there being a thick heavy bank of clouds hanging on the mountain peaks and a thick fog rising from the mountain gorges; the atmosphere being cold and chilly. Last night was so cold that it was impossible to sleep, all the

covering that I had not being sufficient to keep me warm.—
The detachment sent out last night to capture and disperse
the rebels supposed to be a few miles from here returned this
morning not being able to find any man that pretended to
be a secesh soldier. There being only twelve days after this
till our term of service expires, the boys are beginning to
get anxious to get home, there being no prospect of us having anything to do in this part of Virginia. The boys are all
pretty well there not being anything like as much sickness
as there was before we left Buckhannon.

TUESDAY, JULY 16.—The weather this morning is much
the same as it has been for the last eight and forty hours,
cold, damp and chilly. Our Regiment is still laying in Camp
Beverly along with the Indiana 8th, 10th and 13th, and a
part of the Virginia 1st, while the balance of the division is
encamped farther up the valley. We have the rebel prisoners
in our Camp yet, and I cannot find out what is to be done
with them ; some of the boys say that they will be taken to
Ohio and Indiana, and retained as prisoners of war, while
others have it that they will be sent home on parole, which
I think is the most likely of the two. I should think that
something should be done with them soon, and not keep them
here eating up our provisions, when we do not get enough
to eat ourselves. The health of the Camp is extremely good,
there being no sickness of anything worth mentioning; the
boys are all in good spirits and taking the times and events
as easy as possible. There is always an excitement attending
the life of a soldier that has the tendency to draw his mind
from the stern realities of Camp life and which has the effect
of keeping up his spirits under the most trying circumstances, this excitement alone being one of the best friends the
soldier has for keeping him from ennui.

WEDNESDAY, JULY 17.—The weather is still rather unsettled, although it is more pleasant than for the last few
days. Our boys are now looking for and anxiously awaiting
orders to move from this place, and shape their course homeward. We have still forty-two miles to march before we get
to the Railroad, and when that distance is footed over the
boys will feel much relieved in having all their hardships
gone through with. There is nothing going on in our Camp
that is worth mentioning ; there is no drilling done. Since
we have been in this Camp, all the duty that is required of
the boys is to stand their regular turns on guard, and to at-

tend dress parade once in twenty-four hours. The rebel prisoners that we have in our posession are being sent home on parole, they agreeing to serve no more in the rebel ranks during the war ; but for my part I put very little faith in their professions of honor, for I believe the same men that we are setting at large here will have to be whipped at some other place. There were four or five hundred left here this afternoon for eastern Virginia.

THURSDAY, JULY 18.—The weather this morning is clear, the sun coming up looking red and fiery, showing signs that we are going to have a pretty warm day ; the heat already this morning at 9 o'clock being anything but moderate ; we are still in Camp Beverly awaiting events as patiently as possible. The detachment sent out on last Sunday to open the road from here to Grafton returned this evening and report the road unobstructed from here through to that place. The rebels while occuping Laurel Hill, fearing a junction of the forces of General Morris and General Rosencrans, had felled trees across the road for miles between Beverly and Laurel Hill, but at present the road is clear from this place to Grafton. While General Rosencrans with his brigade was cleaning out the rebel Camp at Rich Mountain, General Morris was at work at Laurel Hill, at which place he drove them away from and captured a large number of prisoners, and also a large amount of property, consisting of horses, wagons, tents, arms, and all kinds of army stores.

FRIDAY, JULY 19. The weather still continues extremly warm through the day, but the nights, with their heavy fogs and chilling atmosphere, are cold and uncomfortable, which I am inclined to think is also very unwholesome. There has not been any thing of interest in the Camp this forenoon, but at this time, 3 o'clock, there is something going on that is of peculiar interest to me, and no doubt to hundreds of others that are now gazing on the scene before them. There is always something impressive to my mind in the solemnities attending the burying of the dead, but on this occasion I feel these impressions still more vivid, the circumstance being this: On yesterday afternoon, a musician belonging to one of the Ohio Regiments encamped here, having leave to return home, started on horseback from here to Webster, where he intended to take the cars; but only five miles from our Camp, and almost in sight of our Camp-fires, he was foully murdered, being shot from his horse while riding along unarmed and apprehending no danger near. Particularly to an un-armed man, such transactions speak for themselves, and will perhaps open the eyes of our people who are showing so much leniency to the cursed assassins that we have to do and deal with in this God forsaken country. I am now listening to the funeral dirges that our bands are playing while his comrades are putting his remains in the ground, and I have come to the conclusion that men that would commit such crimes will surely meet with retributive justice from some place, if not from the hands of a justly incensed and loyal people, it will come from a higher power. The cause must be bad indeed when its supporters must resort to such deeds to carry their point in this accursed rebellion. Such deeds are nothing more than could be expected of a set of unprincipled thieves and rogues, such as Jeff Davis has got enlisted in the hell-begotten and hell-hatched iniquity that he is perpetrating against this Government, and which will surely as the Lord liveth, meet with divine vengeance. The men serving in this part of the country will hereafter be less inclined to take any prisoners then they formerly have, but will shoot all found with arms in their hands, retalliation perhaps being the only way that will insure the safety of our men when found in small parties or singly by the cursed rebels.

SATURDAY, JULY 20.—Our boys are still in Camp Beverly, this being the eighth day since we first came here. The weather this morning is likely to change; instead of sunshine we have a dark threatening sky, with every prospect of having a wet day, which is anything but desirable to men placed in the situation that we are, having no other covering but a few yards of canvas, and that none of the best, not being water proof. There were some more prisoners brought into Camp this morning but I suppose they will fare as the others did, be kept here two or three days till they get rested, when they will have their haversacks filled with provisions and be sent on their way rejoicing, that they will have a chance to kill some more of our men particularly when they can find them unarmed. There were some of our dragoons fired on last night from the bushes, and one man killed and wounding three others. Such a warfare is getting rather annoying, but still I do not see any way of putting a stop to it. It is worse than we might expect from the Indians of the Western prairies, and which might alone be

expected from the barbarians of the pampas of South Amer-
ica, or the Hottentots or Bushmen of South-western Africa.
Our boys are very tired of this place, and are anxious to
leave it, but as yet there is nothing definite as to the time
that we move towards home. The Indiana 8th and 10th
move in the morning, and I think that our Regiment will
move to-morrow or next day, or on Tuesday morning at the
fartherest. I had a talk to-day with one of the Indiana
boys who has been at the Rich Mountain battle ground ever
since the fight, and he informed me that the number of
rebels picked up and buried to the present time amounts to
three hundred and thirteen, the number of wounded amounted to sixty making their loss in the aggregate 373, while the
loss on our side amounted to 18 killed and 30 wounded, making a loss of 48 in all.

SUNDAY, JULY 21.—This has been the pleasantest day
which we have had for the last week; there has been a cool,
refreshing breeze all day, making it a great deal more pleasant than it has been at any time since we have been in Camp
Beverly. The boys are getting very tired of this place, and
are anxious to move, which I think we will do the first of the
week. Two of the regiments of our brigade leave this morning
for Webster, on their way home, the Indiana 8th and 10th,
they being the same as ourselves, three mouths troops, and
their time nearly expired. There is no sickness in the Camp
at this time, with perhaps the exception of home sickness,
which is middling prevalent just now. Our Regiment this
morning was asked to stay one month over their time for the
purpose of making a trip up the Big Kanawha river, but
after taking a vote on the question, it was found that the
boys were directly opposed to serving any longer under the
present organization, and therefore refused to go, there being
but thirteen votes in favor of the proposed extension of time,
five out of the thirteen being commissioned officers, who of
course would like to serve longer if possible, it being quite
to their advantage in a financial way, but quite to the reverse
as it regards the men in the ranks; although if it was
actually necessary, I think the boys would all be willing to
go; but all that I have heard speak of the matter, think
that if our services were needed in that quarter, that General McClellan would make it known to us in person, and not
leave the matter in the hands of the officers of the Regiment.
I have heard some of the boys make the remark this morn-

ing that it would be very convenient for the officers to pocket another month's pay, which to them amounts to something nice, while the men in the ranks have the long row to hoe, at the extravagant price of eleven dollars per month, half rations, and the curses and abuse of the officers to boot. But I do not think that the officers will insist on us going, they knowing the feelings of the men on the subject; therefore I think that the matter will be dropped. There has been nothing of any particular interest going on in Camp to-day, more than the burying of a few secessionists, who died in the hospital.

MONDAY, JULY 22, 4 o'CLOCK, P. M.—The weather this day is wet and disagreeable. It commenced to rain at an early hour and has rained ever since; it has not been rain and sunshine alternately but it has been a regular settled soaking rain from five o'clock this morning up to this time, and is still raining. We have to stay in our tents all this day and feel like so many prisoners, not being able to get out long enough to stretch our weary limbs. The water stands in puddles all over our Camp and the mud around our quarters is anything but agreeable. We received this evening the long looked for and anxiously expected order that we have been awaiting with the greatest patience for the last five or six days, the order to move from here to Webster, at which place we will take the Railroad and go either to Benwood or to Parkersburgh, on our way back to Ohio. Our orders are to prepare one day's rations and be ready to move at three o'clock in the morning, and the boys are now prepairing for on early start and a long days march, which I think will go pretty hard with some of them after laying here and having little exercise for the last eight days.

TUESDAY, JULY 23.—The weather this morning is clear and pleasant, the rain having ceased last night about six o'clock. Our Regiment left Camp Beverly this morning at four o'clock, and the morning being cool and pleasant the boys marched off at a pretty good pace, making eleven miles in three an a quarter hours before taking a rest; when the Regiment halted and refreshed themselves with three quarters of an hour rest and a good drink of water, after which we again started and took our course up the winding road that crosses Laurel Hill and at the end of two hours and a half we were on the north slope of Laurel Hill and on the ground that the rebels had fortified so as to make a pretty strong Military post. This Camp and fortification had been the head quarters of the rebel army of North-western Virginia, and was directly under the supervision of General Garnet, at which place he had his head quarters. The fortifications consisted of earth, stone and wood work, in the shape of trenches and breast works, and properly manned and under the command of a skillful officer, would be a strong military post. After taking a rest of one hour and taking a good survey of the old quarters of the rebel army, and a good look at all of their defences, which are now destroyed, we again took the road and after a march of seven miles the Regiment encamped for the night, the boys having marched twenty-three miles since leaving Beverly, a great many of them not being able to go any farther.

WEDNESDAY, JULY 24.—The weather this morning is clear and warm. The Regiment left Camp Barbour, (I name this after the county in which it is located,) this morning at five o'clock, and after a march of nine hours we arrived at Webster, a small village on the Parkersburgh branch of Baltimore and Ohio Railroad, four miles south of Grafton. The Regiment made the march from Beverly a distance of forty-two miles, marching time about sixteen hours. This is the last march we will have; from this place we will take the cars either to Parkersburgh or to Benwood, and from one of these two places we will make our way back to Columbus, Ohio. We expect to leave this place this evening, that is if we can be furnished with a train of Cars, which I think is very likely we will be. There were some of our boys joined us here this afternoon who have been sick ever since the Regiment left Clarksburgh on its first coming into Virginia. The boys all appear to be in good spirits although there are some of them that are pretty well used up by the last two days march. Our time expires on the 27th of the month, therefore the time allotted to reach Columbus is but two days after this, which will be little enough time to go that distance in. There is still talk among the Officers of trying to make the Regiment make a trip up the Big Kanawha but I think that it will be of no use trying, for as far as I can learn the boys are determined to go no farther, they claiming that they have served the State as far as they are bound to do, and as far as their oath compels them to do.

THURSDAY, JULY 25.—The weather this morning is clear and warm. The Regiment left Webster last night at 10

o'clock and after a dismal night's ride in a train of old
freight cars, we arrived in Parkersburgh this morning at
7 o'clock, at which place we lay till 6 o'clock in the evening,
at which time we went aboard of a steamboat and were taken
over to the Ohio side of the river. After we arrived at
Parkersburgh this morning, the Colonel formed the boys into
line and once more put the question directly to them, whether
or not they would make a trip up the Big Kanawha, which
they flatly refused to do, stopping all further comments upon
that question. The Regiment is now lying on the sand at the
water's edge of the Ohio river, and will lay there till there
is a train of cars arrives to take us to Columbus, which may
not be till morning, and if that should be the case, the boys
will have to make their beds on the sand for one night and
make the best they can of it. The Regiment has not drawn
any rations for twenty-four hours, and for my part I have
not drawn any for twice that length of time. I have had
nothing to eat all day and do not expect to get anything till
we get to Columbus, unless there is some person along the
road good enough to give us some.

FRIDAY, JULY 26.—The weather this morning is beautiful.
Our boys lay all night on the sand and gravel by the river
side, without any covering but the clear blue sky and their
old thin blankets, but they all appear fresh and bright this
morning and appear as cheerful as if they had rested on
good beds and under cover of a good roof. We are still laying here by the river side, awaiting the arrival of the train
which we expect every minute. 8 o'clock, A. M.—The train
has just arrived and the boys are piling themselves into the
cars for another long and tiresome ride. We go from here to
Marietta, and from there to Loveland, at the junction of the
Cincinnati and Marietta Road with the Cincinnati and Columbus Road. The distance from this place is more than
two hundred and fifty miles, which distance we have to ride
in a train of stock cars on bare boards, with just room
enough to set straight but none to lie down in.

SATURDAY, JULY 27.—The weather this morning is very
warm. Our Regiment arrived at Columbus this morning at
8 o'clock, after travelling since Tuesday morning, over four
hundred miles, and part of the distance on foot, therefore it
would be no wonder if some of the boys should feel pretty
badly used up, but they all appear to be as well as usual,
except perhaps that some of them look rather sleepy, not

having any rest all last night and rather an indifferent night's rest the night before. We had rather a pleasant day's travel yesterday, notwithstanding the uncomfortableness of the cars that We had to travel in. At the town of Athens, in Athens County, we got some nice bread and butter and cheese, which was a perfect luxury for us after living so long on hard bread and meat, but when we came to the city of Chillicothe, in Ross county, it seemed as if the whole city was at the depot, and such a feast as we had there, we had not seen the like of for many long days. The good people of the city were there by the hundred, with wagon loads, basket loads, and barrow loads of the nicest kinds of provisions to feed our hungry boys. There we got bread and butter, pies and cakes, cheese, ham, beef and mutton, good coffee, and every thing that would tempt a hungry man, and the way the boys pitched in to the good things was fun to see ; every man eat till he was perfectly satisfied and no one went away hungry, unless they were too lazy to eat, which I don't think was the case. After every man had filled his bread basket to its utmost capacity, the boys got aboard the train and we went on our way rejoicing from the fair little city of Chillicothe. After we arrived here this morning and partook of some refreshments at the Rail Road Eating Saloon, the Regiment was marched out to Camp Chase, and took possession of the quarters assigned to them, and where we are now awaiting our discharge so that we can return home. There are now five three months Regiments at Columbus awaiting their discharge, namely : 1st, 2d, 15th, 19th and 20th; therefore, it is very likely that we may have to stay here for ten days before we will be mustered out of the service and paid off so we can return home.

SUNDAY, JULY 28.—This morning the weather is somewhat changed. We are having a very hard rain this morning, with thunder and lightening. The weather in this part of the State has been very dry for the last few weeks, so the rain that is falling this morning will have a very beneficial effect on the growing crops, corn, potatoes and other vegetables. There is nothing of any special interest going on in Camp to-day, therefore there is a scarcity of news. There are a good many troops in Camp Chase at this time, but they keep coming and going so that I cant find out the exact number, but as far as I can learn there is in camp and boarding in the city some five Regiments of returned three months troops. I see it published in the morning papers that the three months troops now in camp will be paid off and discharged this week, and if that is the case our Regiment will perhaps get home the last of this week, it being the last Regiment on the list except one. Our boys are all well and are very anxious to be discharged so that they can return home. This business of laying in Camp is very monotonous; time hangs on our hands and passes off very slowly, making the boys feel very much out of sorts. I have taken up my quarters in the city with a friend of mine and am fareing some better than I have for the last two or three months, but still I am very weary of laying here and waiting, for now that we have got back to the State of Ohio I would like to be released from further obligations, so that I could return home and do some good for myself, for there is no good being done anyone by keeping us laying here at the expense of the State of Ohio. There is very little business of any kind doing in Columbus at this time, and if it was not for the excitement attending the marshaling, dispatching, receiving and discharging of troops, this would be one of the dullest places in the State of Ohio. Business of every kind is pretty near at a stand, except such as is connected with military movements, and that appears to be in a pretty flourishing condition. There is recruiting going on in the city and still appear to be a call for more troops.

MONDAY, JULY 29.—The weather this morning is clear and very warm. Our Regiment is still in Camp Chase awaiting the action of those whose duty it is to settle up the affairs of the returned Regiments. I see no better prospect of our being discharged than there was the day we came here; but all that we have got to do is to wait till everybody is as ready as we are, and then perhaps we will get our discharge. Our boys are all well as usual, but are very tired of this place. There is nothing going on here of any interest, therefore I have nothing to write that would be inieresting.

TUESDAY, JULY 30.—The weather is as it has been for the last forty-eight hours, dry, and very warm, the air being hot and sultry and making any place where there is the least bit of fresh air and a good shade a very desirable retreat. The weather for the last two days has been warmer than I have experienced this summer. The weather in Virginia was sometimes pretty warm through the day, but the nights were always cool, sometimes uncomfortably so, but the days and nights are both very warm here for the last few days, the nights being too warm to sleep with any degree of comfort. There is no news, nor is there anything going on in Camp that is any way interesting, therefore my remarks are naturally very short.

WEDNESDAY, JULY 31.—The weather this morning is clear and still continues to be uncomfortably warm. Our boys are getting so tired of lying here that they are beginning to have the blues, and there is very little wonder, for this is the slowest way of soldiering that we have done since we first commenced the business. There is still a dearth of news in Camp, there not being anything going on that is worthy of notice.

THURSDAY, AUGUST 1.—The weather is still unchanged, it still being hot, hot, hot, and no comfort to be found but in the shade, and no place can there be found but what it is too hot for comfort; the conclusion came to now by the official dignitaries is that our Regiment shall return home immediately without either a discharge or being paid off.— The Regiment this afternoon delivered up to the State authorities their muskets, catridge boxes, knapsacks, haver-sack and belts, and the order is that we will leave here to-morrow morning and return home, and at some other time, perhaps one month hence, there will an officer visit the several Companies of the Regiment at the most convenient pla-ces, and there and then discharge them from the service and pay them for the service which they have performed.— This being the programme that is to be carried out, the Regiment will leave Columbus in the morning and return to their homes, the boys all appearing to be satisfied with the arrangements.

FRIDAY, AUGUST 2.—Our Regiment left Camp Chase last evening and came to the city, and at 11 o'clock in the evening there was a train left the depot taking away five Com-panies of the Regiment. They go as far as Crestline and await the arrival of the other five Companies of the Regi-ment, which will leave here at three o'clock in the morning. The other five Companies of the Regiment left this morning at three o'clock and run up to Crestline where we found the boys that had preceded us and come up on the last night's train. The Regiment was now once more and I presume for the last time all together. Companies A, E, H and G, go east on the Pittsburgh, Ft. Wayne and Chicago Road, while the other six Companies go from here to Cleveland, where there will be another division, Company K will take the Cleveland and Pittsburgh Road and go to Hudson; Companies B and C will take the Cleveland and Mahoning Road and go to Warren, and Youngstown, and Companies D, F and I, will take the Lake Shore Road and go to Painesville, and Ashtabula. At 9 o'clock the train started on their different routes, and the gallant 19th was broken up, after having been together for nearly three months, and undergoing some very hard trials. The boys of the different Companies appeared to me as old friends and I was very loth to part with some of them, but nevertheless the separation had to take place and we are all now on our way home. I wish every man in the Regiment a pleasant journey and a safe arrival to their homes, and if any of them should ever read these lines, they may rest assured that they have the best wishes of a musician that belonged to the Regiment, and shared its hardships and leisure hours. The 19th, from the time it left Camp Taylor till its return to Columbus, traveled over twelve hundred miles, camped in sixteen different camps done a large amount of scouting, was engaged in one battle and captured one thousand of the enemy and killed three hundred, and captured property to the amount of nearly one hundred thousand dollars. The Regiment is now broken up and my notes will have to stop, so good luck to the boys of the old 19th and may every one of them live to see peace once more restored in our land, and the rebels be brought to feel that the Yankee boys of Ohio are always willing to defend their rights, either from enemies without or within the borders of our own Buckeye State; and that their arms are long to reach and strong to strike in the defence of our common country,

www.ingramcontent.com/pod-product-compliance
Lightning Source LLC
Chambersburg PA
CBHW021531090426
42739CB00007B/887